FRAGMENTS GRAVE AND GAY

It was Pope Pius XII who described KARL BARTH as 'the greatest theologian since St Thomas Aquinas'. Certainly he has had an immense influence over the whole course of Protestant theology in our time, and was regarded with admiration and respect even by those who did not share his views. From the time of his *Epistle to the Romans*, in 1919, when he was pastor in a small Swiss village, through the years of teaching in the universities of Göttingen, Münster and Bonn, and finally, after refusing to take the oath of loyalty to Hitler, back to his native Switzerland and the chair of theology in Basle, he was an explosive figure in the realms of both theology and politics. For close on fifty years, until his death in 1968 at the age of 82, he was in the forefront of the struggle to shape a theology that lets nothing of the great past of Christianity go and yet speaks afresh to each situation in our time.

KARL BARTH

*Fragments Grave
and Gay*

Edited with a Foreword and Epilogue
by Martin Rumscheidt

Translated by Eric Mosbacher

WIPF & STOCK · Eugene, Oregon

Wipf and Stock Publishers
199 W 8th Ave, Suite 3
Eugene, OR 97401

Fragments Grave and Gay
By Barth, Karl and Rumscheidt, Martin
Copyright©1971 Theologishcer Verlag Zurich
ISBN 13: 978-1-61097-723-4
Publication date 12/1/2011
Previously published by Collins, 1971

© 1971 of the German original version by
Theologischer Verlag Zurich.

Acknowledgments

'The Birth of God' was originally published in *Wir Brückenbauer*, Vol. XXI, No. 51, Zürich, under the title *'Die Geburt Gottes'*. An English version appeared in the *Deer Park Church Magazine*, Toronto, January 1969.

'The Faculty of Theology' was published by the *Basler Nachrichten*, Vol. CXVI, No. 26, Basle, June 1960, under the title *'Die Theologische Fakultät'*.

'Christianity or Religion?' appeared under the title *'Das Christentum und die Religion'* in *Acta Tropica*, Vol. XX, No. 3, Basle, 1963.

'Atheism, For and Against' appeared under the title *'Atheismus—pro und contra'* in the *Zürcher Woche*, Vol. XV, No. 24, Zürich.

'The "Un-Mozartean" Swiss' was published by *Die Woche*, Zürich, 23. 1. 1963, under the title *'Uns fehlt das Bewusstsein der eigenen Relativität'*.

'Ten Articles on the Freedom and Service of the Church' appeared in *Evangelische Theologie*, Vol. 23, No. 10, Munich, under the title *'Theologisches Gutachten zu den zehn Artikeln über Freiheit und Dienst der Kirche'*. This translation is an amended version of that published in the *Scottish Journal of Theology*, Vol. XIX, No. 4.

'An Outing to the Bruderholz' was published under the title *'Gespräch mit Karl Barth'* in *Stimme der Gemeinde*, No. 24, Frankfurt, 15. 12. 1963.

'A Thank-You and a Bow—Kierkegaard's Reveille' is a revised version of the translation in the *Canadian Journal of Theology*, Vol. XI, No. 1. The original, entitled *'Dank und Reverenz*', was published in *Evangelische Theologie*, Vol. 23, No. 7, Munich.

'Kierkegaard and the Theologians' is a revised version of the translation in the *Canadian Journal of Theology*, Vol. XIII, No. 1. It was first published in *Réforme*, 11. 5. 1963, under the title '*Il y a des théologiens qui* . . .' This translation was made from the German version in the *Kirchenblatt für die reformierte Schweiz*, Vol. CXIX, No. 10, entitled '*Kierkegaard und die Theologen*'.

'Thoughts on the 400th Anniversary of Calvin's Death' appeared under the title '*Zum 400. Todestag Calvins*' in *Evangelische Theologie*, Vol. 24, No. 5, Munich; and 'Karl Barth's Speech on the Occasion of his Eightieth Birthday Celebrations' appeared in the same journal, Vol. XXVI, No. 11, under the title '*Dankesworte anlässlich der Feier zu seinem 80. Gerburtstag am 9 Mai 1966*'.

'Letter to Eberhard Bethge' is a revised version of the translation in the *Canadian Journal of Theology*, Vol. XV, Nos. 3 & 4. The original was first published in *Evangelische Theologie*, Vol. 28, No. 10, Munich.

The Epilogue is a revised version of an article entitled 'A Thank-You for Karl Barth' which originally appeared in the *Canadian Journal of Theology*, Vol. XV, Nos. 3 & 4.

Contents

Foreword	9
The Birth of God	17
The Faculty of Theology	21
Christianity or Religion?	27
Atheism, For and Against	32
The 'Un-Mozartean' Swiss	48
Ten Articles on the Freedom and Service of the Church	54
An Outing to the Bruderholz	71
A Thank-You and a Bow —Kierkegaard's Reveille	95
Kierkegaard and the Theologians	102
Thoughts on the 400th Anniversary of Calvin's Death	105
Karl Barth's Speech on the Occasion of his Eightieth Birthday Celebrations	111
Letter to Eberhard Bethge	119
Epilogue	123

Foreword

' "What came ye out for to see?" An old gentleman who has by far the greater part of his life and certainly of his productive life behind him, and is now in retirement?' Thus Barth described his situation. But it soon became evident that the great teacher's retirement was a very active one. His theological thinking and refreshing humour knew no retirement. 'Seeing the poise and freedom, the humour and vision, the humility and modesty, with which theology is practised here was an unforgettable experience.' So wrote a member of a party of German ministers who were received by Barth in Basle in the summer of 1963.

The contents of this little volume – with the exception of a single item they date from after his retirement from the University of Basle in the spring of 1962 – testify eloquently, not only to his continuing theological activity, but also to his humour, humility and vision. The mere fact that theology can be practised with joy and humour would not merit the translation and publication of these papers. The risk in making available a small volume such as this in English (or any languare for that matter) is that it may do no more than contribute yet another stone to a monument to him. That, however, is as contrary to his spirit as he believed the Calvin monument in Geneva to be contrary to Calvin's spirit. That Barth as a man had humour, joy, humility and gratitude is certainly of biographical interest, but has little to do with what he cared about most, the theme that echoes through these pages.

Barth has been called one of the greatest theologians of the century, and even the greatest. His own comment on that will be found in the pages that follow. Let us therefore refer to him as one of the most outstanding and many-sided theologians of the century. The award to him by the University of Copenhagen of the Sonning Prize, which is awarded to individuals who have made outstanding contributions to European civilization, testifies to his many-sidedness (his speech of thanks is reprinted here), as does the fact that he was asked to cross swords with one of the most renowned German atheists. That he, the leading mind behind the Barmen Declaration, should have been asked to give a theological appraisal of a similar document by a sister church and that, after his retirement from the university, he should have been asked to address non-Europeans on Christianity and religion lends support to the description of him as 'most outstanding'; that the journal *Wir Brückenbauer*, published by the biggest Swiss supermarket chain, should have invited him – the author of the thirteen-volume *Church Dogmatics* – to write a Christmas article for its readers, testifies to his modesty and vision.

No one who ever sat at his feet (as the editor of this little volume did in the last term of his professorship in Basle in 1961-62) could ever write or say anything in his praise that could hope to meet with his approval. What he liked, when one spoke of him, was the admission that through him one had become like him, the foal of an ass, to use the biblical term, that had the privilege of being available when God's Word needed to be carried for part of the way. This was the aptest simile he could find for himself in his reply (reprinted here) to the tributes paid to him on the occasion of his eightieth birthday on 9 May 1966. He regarded all his work as that of a small donkey, a relative of the one that carried Jesus into Jerusalem. That its load was the very heart and centre of theology is also evident from the contents of this little book.

Karl Barth was concerned with 'right theology'. We might call it theological theology, for it is not an automatic certainty that theology is always really talking of God and not 'a deified illusion', as Feuerbach put it. Theology cannot assume the givenness of God; religion can do so, since it is about 'man's arising to go to God'. Right theology arises from the essence of Christianity, from 'God's arising to go to man', as Barth put it in his address to non-European students studying in Switzerland. But if God's arising to go to man is the foundation and content of theological theology, it must unmistakably repudiate many illusory deities or deified illusions. Barth says that Kierkegaard's reveille profoundly awakened him to where the repudiation must be uttered. After Kierkegaard 'going back to Hegel or even Bishop Mynster has been out of the question', he said in Copenhagen. But this repudiation – ever present in a right theology – is overshadowed and outshone by the triumphant affirmation that must be uttered by a theology that speaks of the God who arose to go to man. Barth learnt from experience that the 'truly necessary negations about the subject of theology' cannot be permitted to be effected again and again if the aim of theology is 'to proclaim and to interpret the Gospel of God and thus the Gospel of his free grace'. Thus he had to pass through the school of Kierkegaard and pass out of it and go on to other schools.

But how can a theologian speak rightly of God's covenant with man, the covenant which is the reason why God arose and went to man? Barth's reply is that the explanation of the covenant is not to be found in any general truth, but rather in history, recorded in the Bible, 'the history of God's covenant, the establishment of which is described in the Old Testament and the consummation of which is described in the New Testament, while it now moves towards its fulfilment; the covenant of God with men whom God has chosen, enlightened and sanctified through his Word in the power of the Holy Spirit', as he wrote in his paper on Calvin. 'This, very briefly, was the wisdom that Calvin proclaimed', he said of the man to whose school he went after Kierkegaard's. To both of these, as well as to Dostoevsky, Overbeck, the Blumhardts, father and son, Plato and others, he expresses his gratitude in this volume.

But the history of the covenant, beginning with the testimony of the Old Testament, reaching its consummation with that of the New, and now advancing towards the fulfilment, centres in him in whom God arose to go to man, in whom man sees God's relation to man and man's to God, that is, Jesus Christ. In him theology beholds the truth about God and about man; without him theology would be a reckless enterprise. If Christ is the alpha and the omega of theology, God's true divinity and man's true humanity, then theological theology becomes what Eberhard Busch, my good friend in Basle, who was Barth's assistant from the early sixties to his death, calls 'human theology', that is, a theology that joyfully affirms humanity. In 1956 Barth spoke of God's humanity. He said that God's free affirmation of man, his free participation in man and his free standing up for man was his humanity. In a right theology glory is given to God as to man; because it is given to God, it is for that very reason given also to man. Man is called good and is affirmed because of God; man's humanity and goodness derive from the event in which God manifests his goodness and favour to man. He who understands this event is thankful and joyful, he is truly human man. In an interview reprinted here Barth calls him 'Mozartean man'; he has 'the calm joyfulness so badly needed now in a torn and divided world', the ability to see himself in his own relativity from which true peace comes. He is thankful; his thankfulness is his response to God.

To Barth, the place of the human response to the Word of the God who arose and went to man because of his favour for him is the Church. It is only when it is in that

FOREWORD

place, and nowhere else, that a congregation is a Christian congregation, and it is from that place that it derives its worth. But since that worth consists in responding, it can only follow after the Word of God that has gone before. To Barth, however, to follow after means to serve. God is the God who favours man. He is not served by the congregation when it ceases to see its essence and task in service, to its own people and those around them. This is clearly shown in the evaluation of the 'Ten Articles on the Freedom and Service of the Church' reprinted here. 'The freedom of the Church for service' is how Barth puts it. 'With what else should the Church . . . be concerned other than with its freedom over and against the world about it and its service in that world?' Elsewhere in this volume he maintains that the Church that does not serve represents a crass atheism. 'The atheism that is the real enemy is the "Christianity" that professes faith in God very much as a matter of course, perhaps with great emphasis, and perhaps with righteous indignation at atheism wild or mild, while in its practical thinking and behaviour it carries on exactly as if there were no God. It professes its belief in him, lauds and praises him, while in practice he is the last of the things it thinks about, takes seriously, fears or loves. God is thus turned into an item in the inventory of the contents of an old-fashioned or partially modernized house, a piece of furniture the owner would refuse to part with in any circumstances, but for which he has nevertheless ceased to have any real use.'

Barth here suggests that the Church must always be a serving Church, a mission Church. This was apparent throughout his life, in his continual recalling of the Church to its mission and his own sustained efforts to serve it. No matter what one's reaction may be to his interpretation of baptism (it might be pointed out here that it is utterly insufficient to rely on his 1943 paper, and that it is essential to read *Church Dogmatics*, Volume IV, Part Four, on the subject), it manifests a deep concern for the seriousness of one's participation in the congregation as the people of free, responsible witness to God. (Barth's zeal for a serving but free Church is reflected in his discussion with a group of ministers from Württemberg, reported here under the title of 'An Outing to the Bruderholz'. It appears in connection not only with baptism, but also with the question of war and peace, especially in relation to German rearmament, military service and civil obedience.) Just as God is not God for himself, is not God without man but God for man, so the Church cannot be only for itself, but must live a public, a political life.

The truth of God's favour for man is the content of a certain history; it is not a self-contained principle, applicable to the world or to man, as may be thought fit. That is because this truth is a living and moving thing. This means on the one hand that theology is not a *theologia gloriae* but a *theologia viatorum,* not a theology that has arrived but a theology that is travelling towards its goal, as Barth wrote to Adolf von Harnack in 1923. On the other hand it means that the Church, the congregation, is itself 'travelling', is 'marching on'. The congregation moves from God's favour for man towards God's favour with man. But this favour is still hidden under so much human opposition and incomprehension; it is not yet plainly visible. The assertion that 'God is dead' can therefore be met only by patiently and joyfully believing nevertheless. For the Church has hope, the hope of seeing 'face to face'.

Barth puts this thought beautifully in the paper on 'The Birth of God'. God arose to go to man. From there we come. But 'we cannot invent or create' this. 'But there is no need to do so (though wanting to would be sheer presumption), because it has already been invented for the salvation of the world and every individual in it by the sole Inventor who is qualified to do so, because it has long since been created by the sole Creator who has the power to do so. . . . We should count on the fact that the first and thus the last word . . . has been spoken once and for all.' Thus we should date our transactions, say, ' "in the 1962nd year counting from the birth of God", that event beyond all understanding, that took place, not against, but for the evil world that God nevertheless loves, not against but for wicked and foolish man whom God nevertheless chose to be his brother.'

Karl Barth did not speak the last word in theology. Only he who realizes – without bitterness or resentment – who really has the last word, fully realizes the deficiencies in his own objectivity. Such a man knows his limitations, and can accept them with humour. This is not the kind of humour that takes pleasure in ridiculing others, but the kind that is content to smile at itself, in happy expectation that the word of him who has the last word will most certainly be an inconceivably better one than any that he could ever think of or stammer himself.

The pieces collected here show the smiling Barth. To him the editor owes a debt beyond price. May the thanks of all who owe him such a debt reach him even yet, but only when he is not conversing with Mozart, Calvin or Schleiermacher. (To this list I would add Harnack. On 1 November 1967 Barth wrote me that he 'hoped very much to come to an agreement with Harnack in heaven. The way things stood in those "roaring twenties" made such agreement impossible to find.' The reference is to the public controversy between the two in 1923.)

My thanks also go to the publishers in Germany and Switzerland who gave their permission for the translation and publication of these pieces. They go to Professor T. F. Torrance of Edinburgh, whose patience with me was the second greatest encouragement to proceed with the task. They go to the following members of Deer Park United Church in Toronto: Mr Charles Reid for anglicizing my

German English, to Miss Jane McMulkin, who typed and read all this material, and to my friend and mentor, the Rev. Dr A. Leonard Griffith, who allowed his assistant much time to do this work. To him this little book is respectfully dedicated.

M.R.

The Birth of God

The other day I came across a nearly 600-year-old parchment document, with seal affixed. It was the contract for the conveyance of a house, and it was written in the solemn language that was required in such matters even in those days. The date read as follows: 'Given at Basle on the first Monday after Pope St Urban's day in the 1371st year counting from the birth of God.'

'Counting from the birth of God.' The people of the Middle Ages were not quite so childish as is often imagined, nor were they better or more pious than we. But their thinking and speaking apparently had a dimension which, if it has not been lost, has at any rate faded from our minds. By 'counting from the birth of God', even when money and property, trading and trafficking, were concerned, they knew more than we about the secret of their age, their history and their life.

Whether or not we know about it or think about it, Christmas reminds us of the secret that is also the secret of our age, our history and our life. Christmas is where we come from; that is where everything 'counts' from. It is from there that everything in the economic and political, social and personal, field derives its meaning and ordering, its hidden beginnings and its hidden goal. For it pleased God in his majesty, it indeed pleased him well, to be born and thus become a man. The contrast between this message (the Christmas message) and everything that man might think about God and about himself is very plain.

How is it possible that he who is exalted above everything, is eternal and inconceivable, should have been born and have become a man and that man should have become his brother – and that, once and for all, 1371 years ago, or now 1962 years ago? No special acuteness is required to doubt the assertion, to protest against it as an insult to common sense and experience. But fortunately that gets one nowhere. For this contradiction of everything that man is capable of thinking or believing about God or about himself is in fact proclaimed in the Christmas message, over and above all healthy or unhealthy common sense or certain or uncertain experience.

That message says that the time of gods who were merely sublime, remote and alien, beyond time and space, inhuman, which was also the time of godless man, is over and done with. It even says that it has always been error and falsehood to regard our times, man's history and the world's, as the realms of such inhuman gods and accordingly as the realms of godless men. The Lord of time, of the history of life, has always been, is, and always will be the God who loved, loves, and always will love man, and not at the expense of his divine majesty but to demonstrate it.

Man has always been, still is, and always will be God's partner. The Christmas message tells us that this was established once and for all time, in that God was born a man, became a fellow-man. This God is the true, the living God, in comparison with whom all others (including the most sublime, the most spiritual, the most magnificent) are false, dead gods; and true man is his partner, in comparison with whom godless man is no more than a wraith. 'Ask ye, Who is this same?' Luther wrote in a hymn. 'Christ Jesus is his name, the Lord Sabaoth's Son; he and no other one, shall conquer in the battle.'

Much can be doubted, but not that he will prevail, and not therefore that our celebration of Christmas as the commemoration of his birth should and can be just as glorious a thing as our Christmas hymns declare it to be. 'Gaily let my heart be leaping.' Why has it to a large extent become such a half-hearted affair that nowadays our hearts have little inclination to leap? We are all more or less good and religious. In this respect the usual complaints about man's wickedness and stupidity are battering at an open door.

The trouble is that in our work and recreation, our politics, high and low, our business life, our sports and our dealings with people, and unfortunately also in our church and our family and in other social relations, we go on living year in and year out as if we 'counted the year', not from the birth of God, but from the revelation of some false, because inhuman, god. That means that we are good and religious in the service of gods who are none; we are good and religious in relation to all sorts of ideas, principles and powers that we judge to be divine and therefore respect as authorities, but not in relation to the God who became, is, and will always be man.

What wonder, then, that even with the best will in the world relations between men are so inhuman, hard, stiff and brittle, that a tacit or overt 'cold war' prevails without end? And what wonder that Christmas itself has become a business and a bustle which one looks forward to and then looks back on only with a trace of sadness? Without its secret Christmas cannot be the gay, happy, 'joyous' time of the children's carol.

We are not here concerned with dogma, though we should do well not to be either as casual or as mistrustful about it as people often are. But – and this would be a far better thing – by our praise of the true God and true man (with praise of whom all decent Christmas carols are full), we could let our attention be drawn to the secret of Christmas. For we are not concerned with dogma, but with the secret of Christmas, which is but haltingly indicated in the dogma.

We are concerned with the birth of God, from which we all come, which is the air we breathe, without which, whether with the atomic bomb and other abominations or without them, whether on our old, familiar earth or in so-called cosmic space, and whether we are Communist or anti-Communist, we should struggle helplessly for breath and finally suffocate. We are concerned with letting God's humanity speak to us, the humanity in which his true divinity becomes visible and tangible; with letting it be the vital reality in things great and small; and with remaining within it instead of stepping outside it into the void. We cannot invent or create it. But there is no need to do so (though wanting to would be sheer presumption), because it has already been invented for the salvation of the world and every individual in it by the sole Inventor who is qualified to do so, because it has long since been created by the sole Creator who has the power to do so. We should be simply but seriously joyful about it.

We should count on the fact that the first and thus the last word in humanity's struggle against inhumanity has been spoken once and for all. When we buy or sell we should date the contract 'in the 1962nd year counting from the birth of God', that event beyond all understanding, that took place, not against, but for the evil world that God nevertheless loves, not against but for wicked and foolish man whom God nevertheless chose to be his brother. We are concerned only with doing what we can, that is with letting God's humanity speak to us.

The Faculty of Theology

I have been invited to say something here about the theological faculty of our Alma Mater, which is soon gloriously to celebrate the 500th anniversary of its foundation. To most of our fellow-citizens that faculty is probably a relatively unknown part of our university, and to not a few of them a rather suspect one. In fact, judged by the number of students, ours is the smallest faculty of all. What do we do? There are highly educated people who believe we are concerned with a kind of fable. There are others who, when they hear the mere mention of the word theology, think with a shudder of the burning of Servetus at the stake or similar excesses of which, given the opportunity, we might still be capable today; and there are still others who believe us to be permanently engaged in futile controversy – at any rate among ourselves – about questions that are unanswerable in any case. Finally there are those who take the view that what we are doing is not worthy of the honoured name of science. Small wonder that there was serious discussion in Basle thirty or forty years ago about whether it might not be appropriate to abolish this obscure faculty out of hand. But the proposal did not go beyond the discussion stage. The rector of the university in this jubilee year is a theologian; and in recent years the number of theology students has been much greater than for many years before.

First let me say something about what we really do. Our task, exactly like that of other faculties, consists of professional training, supplying future ministers with the tools of their trade and the knowledge of how to use them. They will need many far more important things in their calling.

But they will need those tools and that knowledge, and we can and must provide them, or at any rate an introduction to them, since the end of their training should not be the end of their studies. They will have to preach Christian sermons, give instruction in the Christian religion, practise a Christian care of souls, and lead, or at any rate give authoritative advice to, Christian congregations. In order to be able to do these things they must above all know the Bible, its languages, its historical formation, its vital message. They must acquire an expert understanding of it and be able expertly to explain it. For this purpose they must have at least more than a smattering of the nowadays very widespread science of Old and New Testament criticism. They must also have a pretty clear idea of what happened to the Bible message through the centuries down to the present day, how it was understood and put into practice here or misunderstood and misused there, and how it was listened to or not listened to in the various phases of world history and the history of ideas. They must therefore know at least the broad outlines of what is called ecclesiastical history. As ministers they will have continually to exercise themselves in independently rethinking the scriptural message in order to be able to pass it on – in a spirit of responsibility to that message and also to the people of the twentieth century. This involves them in a certain amount of exercise in the field of 'systematics', which is provided for them by the study of what are known as dogmatics and ethics. Finally, they must know what constitutes or does not constitute a good sermon, good religious instruction, good care of souls, good work in a modern Christian congregation. They are taught as much as possible about these things under the heading of what is called 'practical theology', which has many branches, like all other disciplines. These are the aims and methods – here deliberately described in rather modest terms – of the part we play in the training of ministers. We also have in our charge young men working for the degree of doctor of theology in the hope of one day becoming teachers of theology themselves.

At this point it seems appropriate to say a few words about theology, its subject-matter and its source. The latter is the message of the Bible, which at close quarters seems to be spoken with many voices, but is ultimately spoken by one voice. It has been heard by many people at all times and in all regions, and it speaks of the dialogue and the relationship that God entered into with man, of the initiation, fulfilment and meaning of this covenant for all mankind. The Bible speaks of Jesus Christ – the name is unavoidable since he is the very essence of it. This source of theology (which can also be called Gospel) is also its subject-matter, to which it is tied just as all other branches of knowledge pursued at the university are tied to their subject-matter. Without it theology could and would quickly dissolve into amateurish excursions into history, philosophy, psychology, and so on. Being tied in this way means that it is no more at liberty to choose its themes than is, say, ophthalmology (theology is incidentally itself a kind of ophthalmology, including occasional operations for opening people's eyes). It searches for the truth (there is only one truth) within its field, within which its various problems are ever posed afresh and by which alone it allows its methods from first to last to be prescribed. Bound to its subject-matter though it is in this way, it enjoys complete freedom of inquiry and doctrine – 'there is nothing between my student's cap and the stars' – and it accepts no instructions or regulations from anyone; it even serves the Church in the independence of its own responsibility. And since the God from whom it takes its name is no dictator, it cannot behave dictatorially. Bound only by his subject-matter, but also liberated by it, the teacher of theology can have and desires to have only pupils who are free in the same sense. If he is sometimes seen in a different light, that may be his own fault, since he is not an angel. But it may be the result of the use of distorting mirrors by means of which distant observers have made up their minds in advance to view him.

But let us return to concrete matters. The work of our faculty takes place partly invisibly, as in other faculties, in our studies, partly visibly, in our lectures, seminars and exercises. In our studies we write our books – and at all events we present-day Basle theologians cannot be criticized for producing too few or too slender volumes – for knowledge of our activities in this field has spread, not only as far as America and Japan, but also actually inside the Vatican. It is to be hoped that, like our colleagues in other faculties, we are honouring the venerable institution of lecturing, which I still think viable, by admitting our students to the living process of our own work instead of retailing from old notes material that they could equally well or better read for themselves in some book or another. But it may well be that a shift of emphasis in the direction of self-training will eventually be desirable in our field of studies. We all, students and teachers alike, feel very happy in our seminar located in the old university building on the Rheinsprung and we are delighted that the danger of being ejected by the stuffed or still vegetating animals of the Zoological Institute seems to have been averted for the time being. Hunched over our texts, we certainly have great need of the extensive view of the Rhine and the Black Forest and also of the smoke-stacks and skyscrapers of modern Klein Basel.

A peculiarity worth mentioning is that the relatively small number of our students to which I have already referred affords us the advantage of somewhat livelier personal contact between teachers and students, and between students themselves, than prevails in the bigger faculties. More problematical is the fact that we teachers live and teach in complete peace (in the nearly twenty-five years I have spent here I have known of only one real quarrel), but without contact or exchange with each other. Another peculiarity of our faculty is its pronounced international character. Of us seven professors, one is a Frenchman, one a Dutchman and one a Swede, while the overwhelming majority of students since the end of the war have been foreigners, primarily Germans, but also many Americans. Rumour had it that some Swiss have not wanted to come to Basle for that reason. But no ill consequences need be expected from this, because in the meantime the theological faculty at Zürich has begun to exercise a certain drawing power on Germans. Ought it not to be an entirely salutary experience for Swiss students, who in later life will spend enough time in a majority among their own kind, to be exposed to powerful foreign breezes during their years at university in their own country? No, we do not want to do without these guests, not those from across the Atlantic and most certainly not those from across the Rhine. On the contrary, we are delighted at the enthusiasm with which they come to Basle, the stimulus they provide, their contribution to our work, and the gratitude with which they subsequently look back on Basle, to which we have many testimonials.

It would, incidentally, be a splendid thing if a not too meagre fund could be provided from which aid could occasionally be given to needy students, who not infrequently live here in very precarious circumstances, to help meet the cost of printing theses, which is an all too painful burden to many, and to make more ample provision for our library. On the occasion of this jubilee, what friendly personality or company might for once think of us as well as of the institutes of the big faculties which are more in the public eye? But it would ill become us as theologians to rest our hopes of good progress in our work on the fulfilment of such wishes. Our subject forbids us to worry about the future. In a bigger or smaller corner of the university –

surrounded by all sorts of justified and unjustified exclamation and question marks, as is appropriate – there will always be a group of young and old 'scribes' who, it is to be hoped, will be at least a little 'trained for the kingdom of heaven' (in accordance with Matthew 13:52).

Christianity or Religion?

An address to foreign students, including many from developing countries, delivered in Basle in 1963.

I have to introduce myself to you as a theologian, that is, as a representative of a branch of knowledge which probably most of you hardly know either by name or by repute. In the universities of many countries it is not taught; and here in Basle and in the rest of Switzerland and Europe the part that it plays is almost everywhere outwardly very modest. At one time, of course, it was outwardly the dominating medium through which all Western academic studies were pursued. That, however, was based on a misunderstanding, and theology has no desire to see a return to this situation. If there is any branch of learning that both inwardly and outwardly can aspire only to serve, it is theology. For it lives on the hidden glory of its subject-matter, not on any reputation based on concerning itself with that subject-matter.

But in this brief quarter of an hour I do not want to dwell on theology, but to try to give you a clue to the very special subject-matter that makes it a special branch of knowledge.

Here in Basle, as in the rest of Europe, you encounter among many other things certain manifestations of the life of what is generally known as Christianity – church buildings and institutions, ecclesiastical agencies and organizations, church-sponsored events and publications, people who profess themselves to be Christians. The Christianity more or less visible in all these things is the special subject-matter of theology. But should you think it worth while trying to see and understand rightly in this matter, beware! Presumably you immediately associate the word 'Christianity' with the general idea of 'religion', and no doubt it represents to you one of those daring but rather doubtful and eerie attempts by man to master the divine by means of an emotional, intellectual or practical leap, the divine being everything that lies beyond his own nature and history, beyond the whole physical and mental universe. Karl Marx was not wrong in regarding religion as an attempt to give the life of the human individual and of human society an 'ideological superstructure' that would explain and help to preserve it. But whenever Christianity has been taken to be one of these leaps or superstructures, and thus a religion, even when it has itself tried to regard and explain itself as such, it has been fundamentally misunderstood. Christianity is not a religion. For whatever is human about it, all the manifestations in which it may resemble a religion, are merely the echo or reflection of a movement that does not proceed from man or have to be carried out by him, but happens to him and has to be responded to by him, a movement by a being of an entirely different kind. Alone among all the religions, Christianity is essentially a pointer, pointing backwards and forwards and in either case upwards, towards the movement of this different being; a movement that differs from all religions, all human leaps and superstructures, and is indeed opposed to all religion.

If Christianity is properly understood, that is, on the basis of the historical sources, the documentation of its origins in the Old and New Testaments – and that, incidentally, is the task of theology – it is impossible to shut one's eyes to the realization that, in contrast to religion, its essence is not man's arising to go to God, but God's arising to go to man. None of the men referred to in those documents engaged in straining their human capacities

CHRISTIANITY OR RELIGION?

to the uttermost, their feelings, intellect, will, and ability, to track down a supreme other-worldly being, or to do justice to him by cruder, or more sophisticated concepts of the divine or by forms of worship emphasizing either the ritualistic or the moral side. Instead they are mentioned only because for their sake and that of the whole world the other-worldly became this-worldly before their eyes and in their ears. The one, the true, the living God – for it is he who is that being of an entirely different kind – arose in his whole majesty and before man ever thought of him or searched for him, or gave him occasion to do so. In his divine liberty he acted, still acts, and will continue to act; he spoke, speaks now, and will speak again, and all in order to take man under his protection, to take his affairs into his own hands and lead him to his goal. In his divine liberty he is gracious. He took part in the this-worldly, terrestrial history from which Christianity takes its name, and provided a unique demonstration of his existence in the man Jesus Christ. Christianity in its origin and essence is still present wherever men listen to the call of this God, are awakened and empowered by him to have faith, love and hope, and wherever they are obedient to him. Essential Christianity consists of – or rather happens when there is – active attentiveness to the acts and word of this God. Thus Christianity begins when religion ends, when religion has been finally overcome. Theology, incidentally, suffered its worst fall from grace when it began to look upon and present itself as the 'science of religion'.

You are visitors to this old Europe of ours, and our good city and university of Basle and the sample fair offers you a vivid picture of its traditions and civilization. Adopt as much of our science and technology, our art and politics, as you can and may. You will also come across signs of what is called Christianity. May they be real signs of real Christianity. And may you not confuse them with the signs of our religion. For, apart from wanting to be Christians and to call ourselves Christians, we are all also religious, at times even terribly religious. There are also religions disguised in the form of science, art and politics, technology, sport or fashion, concealed behind a very demonstrative secularity, which represent superstructures or leaps that are the more vigorous for that very reason, leaps into some sort of beyond, worship of the most diverse gods and idols. Mammon, money, is the most powerful of these concealed but very real deities. Let no one pretend to you that here you are in an area of Christian tradition and civilization, that you are in the 'Christian West'. 'Christian', properly understood, means being governed by the message of Jesus Christ, the liberating discovery of God's gracious move towards humanity. But such discovery is an event, not a condition or institution, and thus is not an attribute with which human creations can be endowed or by which they can be distinguished. Nor are we governed by that event, but at best are only distantly touched by it. The truth of the matter is that we still have really and properly to learn what is involved in this essential Christianity and thus with the happy reversal in which God moves ahead and man follows, God as the father and man his child, in other words the whole meaning of Jesus Christ. There is a religious, but not a Christian West; there is only Western humanity confronted by Jesus Christ.

You too are faced by him, whether you are aware of it or not, no matter where you come from, no matter what open or concealed religion you belong to, no matter what kind of man you may be or what beliefs you may hold. Christ died for all men and lives for you all. The work of God that took place in him and the word of God spoken in him concern all men. The essential Christianity is the horizon and hope of us all. The day may come when it will be better understood and better lived in Asia and Africa than in our old Europe. Meanwhile try to learn, not from us, but with us, that the horizon and hope of us all also includes this: that God is for us and with us, and that Christianity is this happy reversal and elimination of all religion. The morsel of theology that I have offered you is meant to be a stimulus to you at least to think about it.

Atheism, For and Against

In 1963 Professor Max Bense was finally appointed to a chair of philosophy at Stuttgart after the Ministry of Cultural Affairs of Baden-Württemberg had refused the appointment in 1961 on the ground that a declared atheist could not be appointed to a chair of philosophy at a German university. The following article by him and Karl Barth's reply were published in the Zürcher Woche *of 14 June 1963.*

The Necessity of Atheism at the Present Day
by Max Bense

It is not only in Central Europe that atheism is a critical subject, for it is not only there that it touches on three highly sensitive fields of human existence: the intimate emotional world of the individual, including his fear of death and aspiration for a life beyond; the field of beliefs, that is, the possibility of subscribing to them and the ability to do so; and finally a certain party political field connected with traditional, conservative institutions linked with economic interests, social classes and the organization of the State.

But I assume that here I need not be concerned with these critical constants of power. Also experience shows that this subject can seriously be discussed only at a certain level of human intelligence. For it occupies a central position in the 'exertions of our conceptuality'; there can in principle be no unconsidered atheism, no atheism that is not a product of thought; there can be no atheism for which no reasons exist or can be given, no atheism which is pure 'laicism' in fact. Thus atheism is a sign of spiritual human existence and can be discussed only as such. Its reasons and problems are reasons and problems of the intellect; they exist only for intellectuals, i.e. the class of thinking individuals to whom life and the world are interesting and important only from the point of view of the progressive widening of the human spirit.

Thus the vital goal in theoretical exploration seems to me to be the spiritual purity of atheism, and this requires the use of a philosophical language, since in the last analysis only that can do justice to that spiritual purity. Let me mention at this point that the conception of philosophy assumed here is the modern scientific one that does not reduce philosophy to a system or *Weltanschauung*, but instead regards it as the essence of certain disciplines which belong neither to science nor to the humanities but are binding on both. Examples of these are logic, the theory of science, ontology and aesthetics. Basically this kind of philosophy has three tasks: a consolidating task, a critical task, and a Utopian task. The first consists of the analysis and establishment of the fundamentals important for the various positive branches of knowledge, such as mathematics, physics or the study of literature. The second, which has become historically visible and effective at least since the age of Enlightenment, is concerned with the discovery and correction of human and social abuses or ideological habits, institutions, or privileges. Finally, its Utopian task is to draw up new standards, new individual or social aims, to promote the development of ideas that serve the progress of civilization and the unfolding of humanity. Examples of the Utopian function of philosophy are Lessing's 'education of the human race', Marx's 'classless society', Nietzsche's 'superman', and Bloch's 'principle of hope'. So far as the philosophy of atheism is concerned, it must make equal progress along the consolidating, critical and Utopian paths if its present and future are to be justified.

I therefore defend atheism as the necessary and self-evident form of human intelligence and as providing the human meaning of the work of the intellect, assuming man to be essentially the creator of his expandable intellectual world and his reality; and, as I never lose sight of the productivity of the thinking individual, I look at the old double face of human rationality, which gains access to being, the world, essences and things exactly in the proportion to which it grants 'flesh and blood' existence to the Cartesian self, the thinking consciousness, the existing thinker. Rationality is of course to be understood as existential rationality. We speak of the intelligible effect of existence and of the existential effect of intelligence, or, to put it more simply, of the existence-positing power of reason and the reason-positing power of existence.

It seems to me that every description and defence of atheism can and must be embedded in this existential rationality which is appropriate to the idea of man. But two qualifications must first be made.

In the first place, there must be included under the heading of atheism all philosophically stringent descriptions or explanations of the universe as the essence of being that do not rely on a metaphysically postulated supreme being that transcends human thought and experience. This is cosmological atheism.

In the second place, all attempts by man to explain himself as a conscious, thinking and creative being that do not rely on a transcendent, 'different' being must be included under atheism (existential atheism). Thus we distinguish between atheistic theories about the universe and atheistic theories about the self.

Rational and existential arguments can be produced in clarification and support of this.

So far as the rational case is concerned, in the field of

the consolidating role of philosophy, in connection with which they must be seen, numerous arguments have been adduced by the modern school of logicians and theorists of science (Pierce, Russell, Wittgenstein, Schlick, Carnap, Stegmüller and others) that deny all intelligible meaning to all apparent statements about God. It can be shown that statements such as 'God is the supreme being' or 'God is transcendent' say no more, for instance, than does the proposition that 'X is pectable'. In such propositions an indeterminate predicate ('is pectable') is applied to an indeterminate something ('X'). The linguistic sentence makes, not a proposition, but a false proposition. Neither the subject ('X') nor the predicate ('is pectable') is known. Statements about God are easily exposed as such false propositions. They are accordingly neither true nor false. And neither thought nor experience enables us to put anything meaningful in place of the unknown subject or predicate so that an intelligible, meaningful statement results. Even if an attempt is made to avoid these difficulties by explaining that hypostatized expressions such as 'God', 'omnipotence', and the like are merely 'interpretations' of certain basic human emotions, situations and experiences (the fear of death, revulsion from the world, 'total dependence'), we are confronted with the curious situation that in that case very real human facts are co-ordinated with completely empty concepts, so that in order to explain or get rid of our deepest feelings, situations and experiences we are forced to project them into a phantom world, a void. It is true that emotion, which never differentiates sharply enough, may blind us to these complications and illogicalities, but it is also true that the thinking individual cannot for one moment ignore them without being untrue to himself.

It can be objected that thought is in principle an inappropriate agency for the criticism of religious ideas, that 'God', 'omnipotence', 'eternal thought', and so forth should not be the subjects of logical analysis or the objects of scientific inquiry. That argument involves withdrawal from the possibility of thought to the possibility of faith. Thought and faith are then put into a relationship of opposites which can be expressed as follows: Thought is knowing what you are talking about; faith is not knowing what you are talking about. From this it would follow that it would be impossible to say 'I believe in so-and-so' in the same way as one can say 'I am thinking about so-and-so'. While thinking would be thinking only if it were 'about' something, faith would be faith only if it were objectless, and its objectlessness would be a consequence of the elimination of thought by faith. The object relationship of thought corresponds to a subject relationship of faith that can be confirmed only by thought. At all events – and the point must be emphasized, because Kierkegaard and Cardinal Newman made use of this argument in trying to derive the existence of God from the believer's subjectivity – all faith, if it does not refer to an object, is more strongly related to a subject than thought is. The object relationship of thought obviously corresponds to a subject relationship of faith in which believing subjectivity becomes the more prominent the more the objectivity in it disappears.

In summing up the rational arguments for atheism, let me say that it is not in the least concerned with maintaining the non-existence of a supreme being or proving the falsity of propositions about God. Negative statements about God are logically just as meaningless as positive ones, and statements that he is non-existent are just as empty as the opposite. In his consistent rationality the thinking individual is completely an atheist only when he puts the idea of God and all propositions about it in suspense; that is, from the perspective of human rationality which, when applied to faith as the counter-principle of thought, reflects back, as we have seen, to thinking and believing subjectivity and thus posits human existence.

ATHEISM, FOR AND AGAINST

At this point the existential arguments for atheism arise. Let me repeat that the objectlessness of faith, which reflects back to the subjective existence of the believer and to it alone, is the consequence of the fact that faith moves and thinks in unreal propositions, empty forms. But this involves the surrender of the most essential function of the human mind. The thinking individual subjects himself to a restriction, a limitation, of his capacities the reasons for which remain inexpressible and obscure. Thought provides no object for faith, though it is evident that thought is the vital principle of our mind, and that nowhere in its processes does it present us with a prohibition that would cause us voluntarily to surrender the concept of continuity of thought, to drop the criteria of truth and untruth in order to allow a phantom world, a void, to enter into us. The rational situation of the mind becomes a markedly existential one. Either one opts for the theoretically possible continuity of thought, in which case the religious, hypostatized realm of the transcendent vanishes, or one surrenders thought and lets faith take over, whereupon the thinking individual disappears and the whole objectivity of the world retreats behind believing subjectivity.

There are only two ways of avoiding such a situation, which exists, of course, only for those who move on the necessary intellectual level. One either remains at that low intellectual level or must opt for or against the continuity of thought. If one chooses the former, one borders on the unthinking; if one chooses the latter, the choice lies between 'discipleship' or atheism.

Needless to say, a genuine decision can be made only on the basis of reasons which to the thinking being can become arguments of his will, and here three important aspects present themselves in favour of the continuity of thought. In the first place, there is no known principle that would lead us to renounce continuity of thought when it is theoretically still possible, so that there are no reasons for not applying the critical standards of rational, analytical thought to such ideas, subjects or postulates. Secondly, the objective world presents itself to the thought of the existing self, and its vanishing behind the hypostatized content of faith would, at least theoretically, eliminate the existence-positing force of the real human mind. Thirdly, the thinking and willing individual also thinks of himself as a productive, creative, working individual, and in the last resort he can demonstrate himself and the world only in the products of his doing and his work. '*Comprendre, c'est fabriquer,*' said Mersenne, who was known as Descartes's viceroy in Paris. The givenness of the world presupposes its ability to be known, and both imply its ability to produce. But the original blindness of volition and of production can, like the original darkness of reason, be overcome only by thinking, that is to say, step by step with the increase in rationality. Every restriction of this rationality, all attempts to justify a 'mutilated rationality', are liable eventually to turn against the fundamental capacity of expansion of the human mind and its world, which is of course called civilization.

I admit, however, that the opposite choice is at any rate theoretically possible, and that one might opt against the principle of the continuity of thought, and for the possibility of the mind's loss of the objectivity of the world in favour of an immortal subjectivity. But of an individual at the corresponding level of human intelligence who opted in this way one would expect at least the same amount of existential determination as the thinking individual has visibly demonstrated in the world in his decision in favour of the continuity of thought, a decision he made when he connected humanity and civilization with the ideas of progress and technological reality. For faith without the consequences of faith is just as impossible as is thought without the logicality of thought. But forming a view about this comes within the critical and Utopian aspect of philosophy. I do not propose to recapitulate here the mistrust and opposition of the Encyclopedists, Karl Marx, Kierkegaard and Nietzsche, but in conclusion shall simply draw attention to the following.

The anthropological sciences nowadays provide plenty of arguments for the view that the obvious biological frailty of man can be overcome only by taking the step in civilization recognizable in the technological drive, the advance into a man-made reality. The existential category of security, which is based on man's frail life situations, accompanies every process of technological civilization, has its correlate in the rational category of precision, without which the technological structure could not be built. The total process of technological development and the humanization historically associated with it is obviously based on the working out of the existential category of security and the rational category of precision. These are irreversible processes, and every impairment, every slackening, of the power of the human intelligence, every individually or socially introduced or socially effective irrationality or self-interruption of thought, can have only disastrous results. In view of the unfinished state of human civilization, and the frailty and confusion, continually demonstrated in history and politics, of our ideas about humanity, the invasion of methodical rationality into every field of provincial irrationality is an urgent necessity. At all events, it seems to me to be evident that faith and its substrata are becoming less and less important to the intellectual development of mankind and are more and more obviously retreating from the real, historical world, so that there will eventually be no more need of those who cannot make up their minds to apply the analytical and critical standards of the rational intelligence to intimate and transcendent ideas, and are only a stumbling-block.

The Rationality of Discipleship
(Karl Barth's Reply)

Max Bense 'is a man to be taken seriously', a man 'whose arguments are not to be sneezed at'. So wrote the editor of this journal when he invited me 'to parry Professor Bense's blows' and if possible 'refute' him by writing a 'reply' in 'defence of Christianity'. 'Christianity was to be defended.' What am I to say to that? Certainly I take Max Bense very seriously as a fellow-man who obviously cares deeply about his cause, and I hope he pays the same compliment to me. Also his arguments follow logically from his premises, and to that extent are to be respected. But, as I see him striking blows which, though aimed at me, do not threaten, let alone hit me, how can I parry them? Since a man who seriously wants to be a Christian cannot possibly regard as a member of a hostile party a man who obviously does not, how am I to write a reply refuting him? Since a 'Christianity' that, on being attacked by one professor, automatically required a defence by another, would not be worthy of the name, and since real Christianity has always been its own best defence against its assailants and even more against its own defenders, how am I to come to its defence? So I shall not adopt the pose of Hodler's woodman on the former Swiss fifty-franc note, for instance, and write a reply. Instead I shall merely make a peaceful little attempt to state my position.

Max Bense does not think much of faith; indeed, he indicates that he has no use for it at all. But he too believes in something, and pretty vigorously at that. He believes in 'existential determinism', in the pure originality and hence the creativity of the thinking individual, the intelligently active human being who is theoretically capable of infinite progress. But what demonstrable proof has he of the latter's originality and creativity? To prove his assumption, will he too not have to have recourse to 'false propositions' and 'empty statements'? Does not that determinism of his show him to be an outright believer? Should he not therefore be very cautious before claiming to be an atheist and describing himself as such? Does he not attribute to the thinking being a supreme value such as is granted only to a god, and is not this the god that he believes in? Does there not exist in his eyes something in the nature of a church and its creed, the blessed band of persons who live above a 'definite level of intelligence', commune with each other in a definite philosophical language, assure the 'thinking individual' of their fidelity, extol him, and protest against all disbelief that doubts or actually disputes his sovereignty? Bernard Shaw wrote of Charles Bradlaugh, the spirited advocate of atheism in Victorian England, that 'had he been an archbishop, he would have been the most awe-inspiring archbishop that this country has ever seen'.

There are, however, other faiths of this kind, each with its corresponding dogmas, traditions and forms of worship. All of them, like Max Bense's, are directed to a metaphysically postulated supreme being that transcends our powers of thought or experience'. Whether or not they call this supreme being divine, as various forms of paganism, old and new, did and still do, is beside the point. Man, after all, is not only a cogitator. In practice (and also in theory) he may worship the 'god' he is devoted to and reveres in the form of 'existential determinism', and the primitive or refined ideologies of his faith may take the form of 'race, blood and soil' (first in practice and then in theory also), or sport, or fashion, or sex, or money, or – as is very much of the historical moment – technological, economic and political progress. Incidentally, does not the Bible somewhere speak rather harshly of people whose god is their belly? As a glance at the newspaper or outside in the street shows, all these gods have their churches and congregations, their preachers, saints, martyrs, their fathers of the church and their reformers, their high days and holidays, even their popes and their councils. With all due respect to Max Bense's special variety of belief, might one suggest that he pay attention also to the 'disguised religions' of many of his fellow-men who are of a different persuasion from his own? At all events Christians will not refuse to take them seriously – particularly as they will often enough find themselves going a good part of the way with these people's lives and activities.

Or should Max Bense's protest and profession of atheism be directed at these very notable different persuasions, let us say, the worship of Jupiter, Minerva, Venus, Mercury and Mars? If they were, he would find himself in remarkable harmony with the Christian faith, in so far as the latter does not dispute the practical noteworthiness of these Olympians, but so clearly and definitely denies their claim to absoluteness and sovereignty, and their divinity, that the early Christians (if only the same applied to those of later centuries and our own!) were in all seriousness accused of and persecuted for atheism by their contemporaries. But if Max Bense took this line – and how glad I should be if I believed he did – he would have to subject his own faith and his own god also to the sharpest criticism. But he obviously has no intention of doing anything of the sort. In the strength of his particular belief and in the name of his particular god he wants to attack the Christian faith and deny the God that it professes.

Since that is unfortunately the position, it must be pointed out to him in all gentleness that the Christian faith has nothing to do with any subjectivity that involves the renunciation of rationality and produces meaningless propositions and empty concepts and results in the disappearance of the thinking individual; and that consequently the God that is professed by that faith has nothing to do with any supreme being postulated for any reason whatever by man. The Christian faith differs from all other kinds of faith (including Max Bense's) precisely in the absence of that sovereign subjectivity. It attributes to itself neither originality nor creativity; and the God that it professes differs from all other gods (including that worshipped by Max Bense) precisely in that he, his nature, his existence, his work and his word, have never been postulated or dreamt up by man. Any god postulated or dreamt up by man, even the loftiest and most impressive, is alien to the Christian faith and can only be repudiated by it as a non-god.

The God professed by the Christian faith differs from all other gods in that, without assuming any ability or willingness on man's part, but as a free act of grace, he announced himself, to man's deep wonderment, as his Lord, Creator, Redeemer and Father, calling him only to responsibility. And thus the Christian faith, aloof from all spirit of metaphysical enterprise, is merely this responsibility, this free acknowledgment of the self-announcement of God's being and existence, his act and word; free, thanks to the liberation that man experiences as a result of the self-announcement of the free God. This and this alone orders, fills and forms ever anew human propositions and ideas about the Christian profession of faith.

If I understand Max Bense correctly, I think he is afraid; afraid for the rationality and consequently for the 'security' and 'precision' of the thinking individual, and thus for man's humanity. In his position I should be afraid for it too. The excessive valuation that he puts on it cannot possibly assist its power, nor contribute to the so-called independence and autocracy of human thought. Whenever man, no matter in what dimension or by what title, tries to present himself and act as his own redeemer and that of his environment – whether in seizing or expanding external power, or in living out his sexuality, or in acquiring and increasing his material possessions, or as the maker of a new universe of his own on the authority of his own inner convictions, or in the development and putting into practice of a political, technological or economic theory or ideology, or as a thinking individual who engages in abstract, professorial thought – in practice he ends up under the wheels. He may perhaps become 'civilized', but he will surely be dehumanized, i.e. alienated from himself and his fellowmen, changed from a free man to a slave of the spirits' he has conjured up like the sorcerer's apprentice and let loose against himself and the world about him. Then he is at the mercy of all the utterly irrational supreme beings, absolutes, gods and sovereigns, their arbitrary will and their conflict. That is the beginning of chaos, and of that one can well be afraid.

Max Bense need not be afraid of the God professed by the Christian faith whom he wants to deny; he need have no fear for the rationality of the thinking individual, the true value of man's intellectual and sensual, individual and social activity, no fear for his humanity. All this has its place in relation to God, it is intended to be the response to the higher work and word of God which comes forward to meet humanity; it is intended to be gratitude for God's gift, response to his word, obedience to his wishes and commandments – a small but genuine return (with all its insufficiency and error) to him who first loved man. Man can live in relation to this God in the 'existential determinism' of the Christian faith, can in his activities, as in his suffering, take the place that is due to him, and speak (that is, in the form of response) the word that is given to him to speak; or rather, begin to speak it without fear, in spite of all his weakness, folly and wickedness.

In relation to this God 'atheism' is neither necessary nor permitted nor possible (though in relation to all other gods it is very necessary and is required). Man belongs to this God, who is inherently not apart from man, is not against but for him; he is the God of all men, including those who give themselves out to be atheists. How can a man's maintaining he is an atheist alter the fact that God is not aloof or apart from humanity and that his self-manifestation concerns him, too, for his own good?

At one point in his article Max Bense himself refers to the idea of discipleship. Certainly Christian theological thinking is thinking rationally in the wake of the act and word of the living God, the Lord, the Creator, Redeemer and Father, which present themselves to man and ever again show him the way. In the Christian faith and in Christian theology thinking means in principle and practice *thinking in the wake of*. As such, in all the problems with which it deals, it becomes and is an orderly, assured, exact and clear way of thinking in which man is not confounded but honoured. Bense seems to be unable to take anything but a disparaging view of such discipleship. Let him be on his guard. For thinking in the rationality of discipleship, that is, in response, gratitude, obedience, and love, and thus as an act of service and not as an act of mastery, could be not only the principle of theology but also the model for all rational thought, for the pursuit of all knowledge worthy of the name. Bense concludes his article by predicting the disappearance of faith from the 'historical world'. It is possible, so far as the Christian faith is concerned, that this prediction might not come true. It has more than once conquered this 'historical world', and so the light of its 'thinking in the wake of' might shine longer than that of the type conducted on the basis of human autonomy, which is incompetent and impossible in relation to the living God because it is blind. The 'education of the human race' (including the congregation of the faithful on the sunny heights above 'the level of human intelligence') might simply consist of its education to 'thinking in the wake of'.

I have written this, not against 'Max Bense', but — he can protest against this as vigorously as he likes — to a certain extent also in his name. I know the rather sinister figure of the 'atheist' very well, not only from books, but also because it lurks somewhere inside me too. But I believe I know even better the real God and the real man who is called Jesus Christ in the unity of both. He let the atheist depart once and for all and long ago, completely, and that goes for Max Bense as well as for me. Only in our bad dreams can we want to be 'atheists'.

Without any direct connection with the foregoing, and addressing myself particularly to 'Christian'-minded readers of this essay, I should like to add the following in regard to the phenomenon and problem of 'atheism'. There exists in the East at the present time, connected politically of course with dialectical materialism, a rather fiery form of atheism (or of the dream that there is no God), that opposes the Church, religion in general, and thus also what is taken to be the Christian faith, in a more or less militant and aggressive fashion. '*Ecrasez l'infâme*' is its motto. Max Bense is a typical representative of the older, Western, cold type of atheism that is essentially defensive. The universal validity it claims for the negation of faith is based on the alleged sole validity of the scientific and technological method of thought, but in practice it merely claims the liberty to express that claim and, as our example shows, freely to renounce the Church and Christian faith in the name of an intellectual *élite*, 'looking forward to a time when this renunciation will have become general'. Both types of atheism have their special pathos, their special strengths and weaknesses. I should like to say this about them. Atheism is not abominable, because evil, dangerous or pernicious, in either of these forms, even in the Eastern form which is now so greatly feared and therefore so bitterly denounced by the honest Swiss. The atheism that is the real enemy is the 'Christianity' that professes faith in God very much as a matter of course, perhaps with great emphasis, and perhaps with righteous indignation at atheism wild or mild, while in its practical thinking and behaviour it carries on exactly as if there were no God. It professes its belief in him, lauds and praises him, while in practice he is the last of the things it thinks about, takes seriously, fears or loves. God is thus turned into an item in the inventory of the contents of an old-fashioned or partially modernized house, a piece of furniture the owner would refuse to part with in any circumstances, but for which he has nevertheless ceased to have any real use; or rather, which he has very good reasons for taking care not to use; for it might be uncomfortable or dangerous. God is spoken of, but what is meant is an idol that one treats as one sees fit. Who can acquit himself of this third form of atheism? Let all who believe themselves to be Christians consider this: that in this third form atheism is a really evil thing. But this is the form in which it prospers in Christian families, homes (including ministers' homes), groups, associations, institutions, parties and newspapers. This is the form of atheism that is fertile soil for the growth first of the mild, then of the wild, first of the Western and then of the Eastern type, and from which both continually draw their strength. The atheists of the other kind live on the fact that we are not better Christians. So, my dear fellow-Christians, you may well shake your heads over Max Bense's atheism with which we have been dealing here, but 'why do you see the splinter in your brother's eye but not the beam in your own?'

The 'Un-Mozartean' Swiss

An interview with Karl Barth by A. J. Seiler published in the Zürich Die Woche *in January 1963.*

Seiler: Professor Barth, the choice of your successor in the chair of dogmatics at the University of Basle a year ago roused violent controversy. Your pupil Helmut Gollwitzer, now teaching at the Free University in West Berlin, was unanimously proposed by the faculty to succeed you, but he was denounced in a newspaper campaign as a friend of Communists, and as being 'unacceptable to Switzerland' on the ground of his opposition to atomic weapons, his contacts with East European Christianity, and his view that everything is not for the best with Christianity in Western Europe. Even though his writings make it easy to show that he rejects Communism, the attacks on him were successful and he was not appointed. You yourself remained silent, though the campaign against him was indirectly, and partly also directly, aimed at you. Soon afterwards you accepted an invitation to the United States, where you were received with the greatest honours. Your visit created lively interest, not only in theological circles, but also among the public at large. On the basis of your impressions of America, how would you compare the Christianity of that country with that of Switzerland, which likes to think of itself as an especially, or at any rate a very definitely, Christian country?

Barth: I was indeed glad to be able to leave Switzerland behind me for a few weeks after the disagreeable experiences you have mentioned. I do not want to go into the Gollwitzer affair in any further detail, but I must say this. The decision about my successor was extremely disappointing. Gollwitzer would have been a gain to Basle and to Switzerland. As for Christian America and Christian Switzerland, one thing struck me most of all, and that was that in American Christendom the congregation is still a real thing. People do not just attend divine service and then go home again, as they do with us; they do not go just to listen to the minister, but also to be with one another. They 'gather together' for worship. Even in the big cities I visited, such as Chicago, Washington and Richmond, they knew, greeted, talked to one another. Going to church is not a mere private matter; it is a 'social gathering', as the Americans call it. This may have its dangers, but basically it is a good and gratifying thing; the Gospel binds people together. On the other hand, with us the preaching is on the whole better, or at any rate deeper. American Protestantism is still strongly marked by the somewhat superficial reasoning of the Enlightenment movement.

Seiler: I often have the impression that the strongest aspect of our Christianity is the preaching. I am not now thinking of the dimension or depth of Christianity, which is and must remain a matter for the individual; but of the public sphere, the daily round of our social reality. In a conversation some time ago you spoke of a 'Christianity consisting of baptism, confirmation, marriage and funeral services, and at a pinch also of national days of prayer' that is so widespread with us. These things take place on a separate plane of their own, independent of our real life and not affecting it; they hardly touch our social, economic and cultural life. What is the corresponding situation in America?

Barth: My impression is that the fact that American

Christianity is more socially oriented gives it greater practical significance in public life. Though there are no State churches, and in spite of what is to us the confusingly large number of larger and smaller free ones, generally speaking their churches have more influence on secular fields of life than our State churches do – perhaps just because they are free churches and thus dependent on themselves and their members. This influence may sometimes be dubious and give rise to a certain tendency to self-righteousness. But, speaking generally, the impressive feature is the vitality of church life, not least in the dialogue of the churches with each other and with other confessions. In Chicago I spent a very stimulating and agreeable evening with some Catholic churchmen – Jesuits, Dominicans and lay priests. Whisky was offered, and everyone talked completely off the cuff. That has never happened to me, at any rate in Basle. Also in Chicago I was invited to take part in a round-table discussion with a Jesuit, a Jewish rabbi, a liberal Protestant, an orthodox Protestant, and a layman. It took place on five evenings in a single week in the huge Rockefeller Memorial Chapel, and we had an audience of between two and three thousand people every evening. Imagine that in the Grosse Musiksaal in Basle! Again the discussion was completely frank. The differences that of course came to light were neither hushed up nor exaggerated, but were passionately and yet objectively argued. It was precisely the 'let's get together and talk' of which we talk so much.

Seiler: As the Gollwitzer affair showed, we in Switzerland have totally forgotten about this 'getting together and talking', particularly in politics and foreign affairs. The theologians and ministers whose Christian convictions caused them last March to come out in favour of the prohibition of nuclear arms were and are still denounced as 'the gravediggers of the Western world' and the like. What is the origin of this atrophy of genuine public discussion, this unchristian lack of political generosity? And why do our Christian churches on the whole shrink back from taking up clear and unequivocal positions on such vital issues as nuclear armament unless they are forced to do so? The result is that such a convinced Christian as the Catholic historian Friedrich Heer has said that the actions of the Church today generally bear the stamp of reaction.

Barth: Yes, how has it come about that in Washington I was able to have a far more open and uninhibited political discussion with some of the men close to Kennedy than I could have here with certain of my theological colleagues? Why did I meet no one in America who had any sympathy for the Gollwitzer affair or understood the decision of the city of Zürich to refuse Oistrakh permission to play there? Why did Swiss Protestantism take a stand on nuclear armament only when it was forced to do so by the imminence of a plebiscite? Perhaps we must go back to the situation of the German Church under the Nazis. At that time a regeneration took place in the 'Confessing Church', there was a revival of testifying to Christ. The post-war political restoration was accompanied by a church restoration that led to a reciprocal alliance. In Switzerland the situation was similar, with the qualification that with us during the war the Church assumed a position of spiritual resistance only to a very limited extent. After the war it found absolutely no more spiritual tasks to do. The Church is always sick when it is without a task.

Seiler: Looking at the Nazi period, I often think there is an element of exorcism in the attitude of the Swiss to foreign politics, as if during those years we got used to having the Devil, not just painted on the wall, but right on our frontier. We have now carried that attitude over to the world split between East and West, and forget that the ink-bottle has become an atomic bomb and thus a boomerang that will come back and hit us.

Barth: Above all, the Devil today is a long way away. We should show ourselves in our true light only if the Russians were on Lake Constance. Might a Red Pilet-Golaz not appear then? But as for exorcism, shortly after the Hungarian rising a very dear colleague of mine preached in Basle Cathedral on Matthew 8:29 ff., which describes how demons were driven out of some men possessed and into a herd of swine. He preached well, indicating that one day the demons would be driven out of the Kremlin too. Afterwards I reminded him that he had forgotten something, namely the swine into whom the demons entered. In such cases it is often we who are the swine. What I mean is that one should guard against driving out of others demons from which one is not free oneself, or against which one is not proof. This applies particularly to a nation of born pedagogues such as we Swiss now are. We like getting up on the platform and telling other people what to do. This is being shown again now in our very unchristian pride in relation to the Italian and other foreign workers whose labour we find useful enough in keeping our economy booming. It also appears in our ostrich policy of refusing all contacts with the East. Though it has been clear since Kennedy's assumption of office that a slow but distinct relaxation of tension has been taking place on the world political stage, and a *rapprochement* between East and West, we Swiss are more Western than the West and talk about abandoning our neutrality. If we go on like this, we shall end up by looking like the village idiots of Europe. Since 1945 the mission of Switzerland should have been to stand *au dessus de la mêlée* and build a bridge between East and West. That would be a truly Christian mission. But we Swiss lack the Mozartean element, the calm joyfulness so badly needed now in a torn and divided world. We lack the ability to see ourselves in our own relativity – it is that from which true peace comes. So in many respects all that remains is retreat into silence – and the hope that in it forces may be at work that are the agents of common sense and real Christianity.

Ten Articles on the Freedom and Service of the Church

I. Text

'Looking to Jesus the pioneer and perfecter of our faith, who for the joy that was set before him endured the cross, despising the shame, and is seated at the right hand of the throne of God. Consider him who endured from sinners such hostility against himself, so that you may not grow weary or faint-hearted.' (Hebrews 12:2-3.)

There is only *one* Lord – Jesus Christ. Through him, God created us and all creatures. In his death and resurrection, God has reconciled the world to himself and made him to be Lord of lords. Through the Holy Spirit we are God's children. We wait patiently for the perfecting of his kingdom in glory, and know that we must all appear before the judgment seat of Christ. In this confession of faith stands the freedom of the Church, its service and its future.

1. The commission to preach. Jesus Christ sent his Church into the world to proclaim God's reconciliation and to attest God's will to all men in all spheres of life. The acceptance of the Gospel does not place men under an oppressive dictatorship, but brings them rather into glorious liberty. Refusal of the Gospel means remaining under God's judgment. God wants us to proclaim his Gospel confidently, neither fearing nor seeking to please men. Not even the past or present failures of the Church can cancel this commission. Repentance is not a paralysis *vis-à-vis* guilt; it is rather a better obedience to the commission. The Church can trust the inherent power of the Gospel.

We lapse into unbelief when we imagine that we must

use the Gospel of God to achieve recognition and honour for ourselves, by turning it into a means of aiding and confirming our earthly aims, or by adopting the specious view that particular social orders in themselves make possible the obedience of faith – yes, that they even bring to fruit what that obedience demands.

We disobey our Lord's command and fail to love our neighbour if we withhold the comfort of the Gospel from troubled consciences, but also if we remain silent about contemporary sins. When the Church shrinks from attesting God's will in every sphere of life, then even its preaching of the forgiveness of sins becomes restricted and ineffective.

2. *Life in faith and obedience.* God wills the new man created in his image. That is why he reconciled us to himself in Christ. He has renewed the dignity which man lost by his fall and has given meaning and fulfilment to our life. That is why he calls us to renounce all idolatries, to show in our life the power of reconciliation, and to serve our fellow-men in all areas of life. We must discover in whatever social relationships prevail what God's will is for us and do what is good in his sight.

We lapse into unbelief if we imagine ourselves forsaken by God in the circumstances surrounding us and so fall into despair, or if we interpret the given historical and social factors as direct expressions of God's will and so accept them unconditionally. In the freedom of our faith we may not renounce on principle the duty of distinguishing between the service required of us for the maintenance of life and our refusal to become bound to atheism.

We act disobediently if in our worship we confess that God is the Lord of our life and then, in our daily life, accept the absolute claims of an ideology and thereby withdraw from obedience to the absolute demands of the first commandment. We are disobedient also if we allow ourselves to be bound to a morality determined by an atheistic *Weltanschauung*, in which man apart from God is made the aim of education and culture. We confuse men's consciences if we do not reject the view that God's laws and the so-called 'ten commandments' of socialist morality have the same humanist ends in view.

3. Science and truth. God, who has revealed himself in Jesus Christ, is Creator and Lord of all things visible and invisible, not a part of that being to which the world belongs. Faith in God the Creator frees us from all mythical interpretations of the world and enables us to investigate scientifically the whole of that reality in nature and history which is open to our sense-experience and reason, without falling victim to any ideology of science. It is appropriate to want to understand this reality in its coherence without bringing in God as a stop-gap where our knowledge is as yet imperfect. It is, however, not appropriate to deny both the basis of scientific freedom and its limits by denying God and by claiming that the knowledge acquired within these limits is the one all-embracing truth which answers all questions, including the basic questions of human existence. Only in the confrontation with Jesus Christ does the truth about man and his destiny as God's partner and neighbour to his fellow-man emerge. He sets us free to receive our life and our world for what they are, namely God's creation entrusted to us. We act unbelievingly and disobediently when we despise or mistrust reasonable scientific inquiry or when we absolutize its methods and results, thus evading God's truth and our responsibility to him.

We act unbelievingly and disobediently when, for whatever motive, we distort, falsify, or suppress the facts about our life in nature and history.

4. Justification and justice. In the cross and resurrection of Jesus Christ, God has declared lost man to be righteous and has called him to live as God's new man in his kingdom. To that end God, in his preserving goodness, sustains the world and protects man in his humanity also by the order of human justice.

It is true that one cannot deduce orders of justice valid for all ages from God's righteousness. Yet that righteousness demands that all earthly justice respect the dignity of man created and redeemed by God, uphold the equality of all before the law, assure the protection of the weak and allow room for the proclamation of the Gospel and the life of love for one's neighbour.

In spite of his sin, man can establish viable forms of justice. But in his opposition to God who demands justice man continually succumbs to the temptation to pervert justice to his own selfish ends or to subordinate it to the absolute claims of some ideology and thus to destroy it. Where there is no mercy, there is also no justice.

The Gospel of God's righteousness and the commandment to love one's neighbour commit the Church to a concern for earthly justice. Such concern shows itself in the witnessing to God's commandments, in the demonstration of common humanity in earthly vocation, and in the willingness to suffer injustice rather than commit unjust deeds.

We act unbelievingly when for the sake of some ideal justice we do not take seriously the existing law in all its relativity, or when we regard the striving for a reasonable law as futile in view of the power of sin.

We act disobediently when we silently tolerate the misuse or destruction of the law because of some political or economic end and when we do not speak up on behalf of our neighbours and suffer with them when justice is being denied them or their human dignity is threatened.

5. Reconciliation and peace. God has made peace with the world through the crucified and risen Lord. Christ is our peace. His Gospel announces the beginning of a new humanity in which enmity between men and nations is done away with. For this reason Christians are to be ministers of reconciliation in the world.

This ministry commits us to seek peace also in earthly relationships. Even when this puts us between opposing parties in a peaceless world, we strive, each in his place, to work reconcilingly and to establish peace through appropriate decisions and acts. We renounce hatred and the desire for revenge because they go against God's reconciling will. Nor do we participate in the vilification of an opponent's honour.

The ministry of reconciliation also commits us to work honestly and earnestly for peace among the nations. In view of the means of mass destruction war is less than ever a possible solution of political and ideological tensions between nations and power blocs.

The Church acts on behalf of those who on grounds of religion and conscience object to military service just as it recognizes its pastoral responsibilities to those of its members who take up arms.

Whoever has to suffer on account of his ministry of reconciliation may be certain of God's faithfulness and shall know the help and interceding love of the Church.

We act in disbelief when we confuse earthly peace with that of God, and when we measure our work for earthly peace in terms of human ideologies, political ideals or thoughts of reprisal, or when we give up in despair our commission to sow peace.

We act in disobedience when we do not resist the mistaken equation of political or national self-interest with the service of peace.

6. *Work*. God has commanded that we use the gifts of creation, entrusted to us by him, in responsibility before him. This applies very much to our work too. Our work

is to be a service to our own livelihood and to that of our fellow-men. In this service we are to honour God. This command of God lends to work its dignity and proper measure. But since our life stands under the curse of sin, our work is also a toilsome burden which we only make heavier to bear when we regard it as a means of self-redemption. Jesus Christ makes us free from the idolization of work. It is not his will that man should become the slave of work. He helps us to order work, leisure and prayer aright. Under his blessing we can serve one another with our work, praise God and be faithful in work which is unsatisfying and apparently useless.

We act unbelievingly when we mistakenly suppose that work made man and that it can even redeem him, or when we despair of its significance because our illusions have been shattered.

We act disobediently when in our work we relinquish or become indifferent to our responsibilities, or when we cause hardships to our neighbour by acting selfishly or deriving advantages at his expense.

7. *The State and its authority.* The Church confesses Jesus Christ as Lord, to whom all power in heaven and earth has been given and who is Lord also over those who possess earthly power. By God's ordinance these rulers have to make sure that peace and justice prevail. We honour this gracious ordinance of God by praying for the State and by respecting its authority.

Earthly rulers remain under God's commission and in his hand even when they fail to carry out this commission, when they make themselves the rulers of men's consciences and invade the sphere proper to the Church. On the basis of this conviction we must witness the truth to the State, even if that means suffering in consequence.

We lapse into unbelief when we do not acknowledge in gratitude this ordinance of God, or when we imagine that a State, amiss in its divine commission, could put itself outside God's sovereignty and need no longer serve him.

We act disobediently when we do not examine where in the State we can best serve the preservation of life in accord with God's will. We act disobediently when we do not stand up for the truth, when we remain silent about the misuse of power and are not ready to obey God rather than men.

8. The life and service of the Church. The Church lives only because Jesus Christ, in the Holy Spirit through his Word and Sacrament, gathers men together as his congregation, binds it to himself and sends it into the world as his witnessing community. Until the coming again of its Lord, it is on the move: oppressed from without, tempted from within, and outwardly poor. But precisely in this way is it the body of Christ and thus even today the locus of his redeeming presence. Its life consists in its confidence in the Lord, in its obedience to his command and in its reliance on his promises. Because he wills the Church, it shall remain. It receives as a gift from its Lord the living space and the legal recognition which it possesses at various times of its history. When the Church upholds its right in the world it upholds the freedom to preach and to serve. Its sole obligation is to its Lord's commission; in no historical situation is it relieved of its commission. This it will carry out in ways old and new. It will encourage its members to fulfil this service in accordance with the measure of their natural and spiritual gifts and find opportunities for them to do so. The sacrifice needed for the fulfilment of its service the Church will also furnish.

The Church acts in unbelief when it is concerned with the safety of its life in the world, when it shuns suffering which arises out of its discipleship of Christ and when it is intimidated by prognoses which are contrary to the promises of the Lord.

The Church acts in unbelief when it becomes lazy, retreats behind the walls of the church buildings, or when it leaves the responsibility placed on all members of the congregation to individual people, groups or organs of the Church. It is equally disobedient when it seeks to secure its effectiveness in the world by relinquishing its proper task.

9. The order of the Church. By its message and its order the Church must demonstrate that it is its Lord's own and that it wants to obey him. It is true that it cannot simply read from Scripture what its order is to be now and for ever; the form of the Church is subject to change. Yet, even allowing for historical circumstances, the Church must conform to its essence, must not contradict Scripture, and must serve the fulfilment of its commission. It is therefore part of its responsibility to its Lord to determine its order.

The Church lapses into unbelief when it trusts some order to do what only the Holy Spirit's activity can do, and consequently, instead of seeking opportunities of true service, clings to traditional privileges for its own sake, or when it abandons the form of its order to the changes in the prevailing forms of society.

The Church is disobedient when it dissolves its order for arbitrary reasons, when it does not keep to its own order, or when it surrenders the forms of its order to requirements imposed from without.

10. The hope of the Church. The Christian Church confesses the victory of its Lord as the decisive, though hidden, reality in the world and history. This gives it a confident expectancy of the end, strengthens it in its service and struggle in the world, enables it to bear patiently the sufferings of this age, keeps it from all false activism and confirms it in sober activity day by day. The Church waits alertly and prayerfully for its coming Lord and proclaims the Gospel to all men until he makes plain his lordship. Trusting in this, it turns away from all ideas and plans for man's self-realization, warning all men against any attempt to redeem themselves by their own efforts. What is born of the flesh is flesh, and the kingdom of man is never that of God. The world revolution, therefore, can never be the final decision, nor the new man in the new society the fulfilment of history. Whatever is in store for us is already decided in Christ's victory.

In this confidence the Church helps within the frame of the humanly possible to overcome the sufferings and cares of the world and to replace the worse by the better. It knows that all human endeavour is provisional and imperfect. It waits for the day when what it believes even now will be plain to the whole world: 'The kingdom of the world has become the kingdom of our Lord and of his Christ, and he shall reign for ever and ever.' (Revelation 11:15.)

II. An Evaluation

The Conference of Evangelical Churches in the German Democratic Republic recently published a document containing ten articles about the freedom and service of the Church. I have been asked to say whether one may discern in it 'the direction given to the Church today by exegesis of the Scriptures and the Creeds' and, if so, to what extent. This question excludes discussion of the relationship between these articles and the problems faced by Christians and the Church in that country today. I know those problems only from afar off and in a general way. We shall concern ourselves with the articles as guides for Christian and ecclesiastical service; in this respect this document could and should claim attention and validity at other times and places also (if not at all times and places).

FREEDOM AND SERVICE OF THE CHURCH

1. The ten articles are prefaced by a statement resembling a confession of faith. It is followed by the articles, dealing individually with the following matters: Article 1, the commission of the Church, which is the proclamation of the Word; Article 2, the personal life of faith and obedience demanded of the Christian; Article 3, the relation between truth and science; Article 4, the relation between 'justification' as the divine and 'law' as the human order of life; Article 5, reconciliation and peace (peace among nations seems to be meant especially); Article 6, the value and dignity of human labour; Article 7, the sovereignty of the State and its limits; Article 8, the life of the Church in the world, the life that is uniquely hers in relation to her origin and commission; Article 9, her order; Article 10, the coming of Jesus Christ as the hope on which the Church is founded and by which she is sustained and guided.

The authors of this document did not intend it to be a confession of faith; the comments accompanying and elucidating the individual themes would indicate that. (If it appears to be such, it is merely incidental.) Nor is it intended as an address to people outside the Church or the officials of the State or party. (If it appears to be such, then that again is merely incidental.) It is rather directed to the congregations, especially their ministers, as a pastoral and theological guidance for their attitude towards and behaviour in the circumstances that shape their environment and thus affect them too.

With this in mind, the ten articles treat of the freedom and the service of the Church. As the title indicates, the area of concern is twofold. On the one hand, the aim is to summon to original and thus autonomous Christian and ecclesiastical thought, speech and action that unambiguously identify and delimit themselves as such and reject all optimistic accommodations, co-ordinations and identifications of the Church and the world based on merely practical, or, in the manner of Richard Rothe, on speculative considerations. On the other, it is a call to responsible Christian involvement and participation in the context and the givenness of the civil and social order, the operative ideas and trends in which Christians find themselves. Withdrawal inwards into a piety or a 'churchiness', founded on pietistic or politically reactionary motives, is condemned. In particular, the elucidatory comments (about disbelief and disobedience) indicate this double orientation of the document. In one way they speak eminently of the freedom, in another of the service, of the Church.

Their formal and material resemblance to the six articles of the Declaration of the Synod of the German Evangelical Church held at Barmen in 1934 cannot be overlooked; nor can the difference between them. They are alike in so far as the Church at Barmen also undertook to clarify its place and function at a given point of time. They differ in so far as a confession of faith was intended at Barmen and only incidentally and indirectly a refutation of the one error that threatened the Church at that time and had already partly divided it. The Synod of Dahlem, held in November 1934, outlined what in the ten articles is meant to be an indication of the way to be followed, but then it had a distinctly canonical character, entirely lacking in these ten articles.

If one wishes to do justice to these articles, this intention and the way in which it is worked must be borne in mind.

2. It seems to me that several criticisms of the articles do not do them justice. That entitled 'No Liberating Faith' obviously demands too much of them. If Barmen 1934 had a certain liberating effect, it was certainly not due to the faith expressed in the six theses and antitheses; it was rather their source, their object and content that led to the liberation. Other similar criticisms make me suspect that they are based on certain suspicious assumptions rather than on

an honest exegesis of the ten articles. I do not wish to deal with criticisms that seem to me to be too canonically or politically oriented. Let me cite just one example: Article 4 was said not to have avoided the hazard of slipping into a Roman way of thinking in terms of natural law, in spite of all safeguards. Let me assure the reader that my eyes are still very keen in this matter, but with the best (or worst) will in the world I was not able to discover any such hazard in this paragraph.

So I think I can begin by saying with a quiet conscience that the ten articles are good guidance to the Church, its members and leaders. I found not one statement in them to which, either individually or in its context, I could or should raise any theological objection, that is, in the light of Scripture or the Creeds. I prefer to believe that the way in which these articles speak on the two fronts mentioned is substantially correct and important. With what else should the Church there and today (as everywhere and always) be concerned other than with its freedom over and against the world about it and its service in that world? Also I could mention a whole series of statements in this document that I consider especially significant and remarkably formulated. At the end of Article 7, for instance, there is the statement that, if the congregation does not bear witness to the will of God in every field of life, its preaching of the forgiveness of sin deteriorates and becomes unfruitful. Again, Article 4, paragraph three, says that where there is no mercy there is also no justice. Then there is the statement in the middle of Article 5 that in view of the means of mass-destruction war today is less than ever a possible solution of political and ideological tensions between nations and power blocs; and the statement at the beginning of Article 7, unequivocally declaring Jesus Christ to be the Lord also of those who hold civil power; and the opening of Article 8, declaring that the Church lives only because of Jesus Christ's gathering and uniting of men as his congregation and his sending the latter into the world through the Holy Spirit; and finally the beginning of Article 10 (which is very beautiful and clear also in other respects) which speaks of the already accomplished victory of Jesus Christ as the 'decisive, though hidden, reality in the world and history'.

The ten articles should, in my opinion, be looked at in the light of (1) their truly biblical and Reformed tenor, and (2) the luminous statements referred to above and others similarly luminous. Needless to say, they take us spiritually, intellectually and theologically into a world very different from that of Luther's Catechisms, the Heidelberg Catechism or the Confession of Faith of La Rochelle. One would, however, have to be short-sighted or too quick-sighted to overlook the fact that in their own way and their own time they are intended to point in the same direction as that in which those old documents, and the Barmen Declaration in this century, tried to point. *In magnis voluisse sat est*. If only the Church everywhere (including the West) had so much good guidance through the strait between Scylla and Charybdis. Let him who is dissatisfied give the Church better guide-lines – with the same purpose and orientation. Meanwhile let him follow this guidance.

3. Nevertheless I have already indicated that I too do not regard the articles as altogether the ideal guidance to be given to the Church today. In my estimation, going so far as to claim ecclesiastical 'authority' for this document, as has been done in several quarters, has done dubious service to what is at stake here. To have such 'authority', it would have to have behind it, not only the consensus, certainly remarkable as such, of the Church leaders of the German Democratic Republic, but also synodal backing; and, even if it had such authority, it would have been better not to

declare that it had (no one, so far as I know, made any such declaration at Barmen), but to have left it to the inherent power of the document to convey that it did in fact possess it.

Having expressed my basic acceptance and praise of the ten articles, I shall not withhold the criticisms that have occurred to me. The errors I see in these articles, however, are in my view not incorrigible.

One can tell from the language, the conceptuality and the arrangement that much diligent, but rather extended work was done on them by many different hands. Analytical investigation, with the rules of which I am not familiar, would produce much evidence for this. Things, instead of being stated once and in the right place and in a precise and axiomatic fashion so that they provoke reflection, are repeated in different contexts and with all kinds of expansion, supplementation and abbreviation to prevent them from being overlooked. This has an adverse effect on the style as well as on the force of the statement. Quite formally, I miss something in the nature of co-ordination and purpose in the articles which would have rendered them more impressive to the reader – and perhaps also to those *extra muros ecclesiae* who were interested. Would it not have been possible, for instance, to combine Articles 4, 7, 8 and 9 into one article?

This literary deficiency is reflected in a lack of substance. I wish that these ten articles, to which I have no essential objections, had been given a much greater theological concentration. Should the preamble about proclamation not be very much more than a mere preamble? Should it not much more effectively dominate, determine and permeate the whole? Should the excellent Article 10 about hope, based on the already accomplished reconciliation, not have been written in at that point and thus have provided the decisive, fundamental statement of the whole document? Would Matthew 5.13 f. ('You are the salt . . . the light . . . a city set on a hill . . .') not have been preferable as a New Testament preface to Hebrews 12:2-3, in a document in which the Church is spoken of as the Church in tribulation? This, though pertinent, is stated somewhat prematurely and too abruptly here. Why does the title of the whole not speak of the 'freedom of the Church for service', instead, as it does, of its freedom and service in that unresolved separation of the two? Could not and should not the inner relation between these two positive and critical main themes, which the sympathetic reader will by now have discerned, have been made plainer to all readers? If that had been done, it would have avoided the impression being given that, in spite of the recognizable desire to keep the two in balance, the emphasis lies more on the defence of the freedom of the Church than on the explanation and injunction of the necessity of service. It would have been plainer that the Church with its 'yes' and 'no' (to the Right and to the Left) – far from having to struggle painstakingly against the various foreign streams – is actually borne and moved by that inclination given to it in its foundation and commission. Also this would have allowed the formally somewhat confusing and fatiguing differentiation between disbelief and disobedience, which in the last analysis is biblically untenable, to be dropped. Instead, the obedience of faith, which is also more positive, could have been talked of. Several of the sighs, appropriate and understandable as they are, would have faded out before the joyous roar of the Lion of Judah had the statement that Jesus Christ is the Lord of the world and of the Church not only been expressed, as it was, in nearly every article in one form or another, but also lived out with a fundamental confidence, reflecting the conviction and faith behind the words, in the sight of the frightened and confused within and the self-confident devotees of progress without. What was said about the 'outside' world, Socialism, etc., would then have

been more helpful and hopeful, besides showing greater
involvement in it. In regard to the State, the things said
about it would in turn have been more in the spirit of a
deeper, inner respect and a greater responsibility. (When
will that disagreeable word authority [*Obrigkeit*], with its
patriarchal chill, finally disappear from the Christian vocabulary?) There would also have been more compassion and
mercy in what was said about atheistic propaganda, which
misses God's existence by so much and is therefore funny.
Conversely, one may ask whether there should not have
been a direct or indirect attempt to 'overcome the past',
perhaps in the form of an answer to the somewhat contrite
question why in earlier days, when outwardly it was more
prosperous even though the inner uncertainties of its
existence were much more dangerous, the Church did not
find it necessary to issue such critical directives – a question
that arises most naturally in view of the circumstances
in which this document was issued. I think that what is
missing from it as it stands would have sharpened rather
than dulled the incisiveness with which it is necessary to
speak in that part of the world today – as indeed everywhere and at all times – to those on the Right and those
on the Left. But in this case a more strongly Christological-
eschatological concentration and expansion would have been
necessary to meet the requirements. And finally, if the
document had been more powerfully and completely a
confession of faith, this would not have adversely affected
its character as a guide-line.

It remains for me now only to express my hope that neither
my presentation nor my praise nor my criticism of the ten
articles have provided grist to any mill, for that is really
not my intention; grist neither to the mill of the assimil-
ators nor to that of the *attentistes* or reactionaries who, I
understand, are likely to be identified in a reference to two
well-known bishops over there. I shall have been correctly

understood if there transpires in all that I have said my hope and confidence that the Church in the German Democratic Republic – and not only in the German Democratic Republic – will continue courageously and humbly, circumspectly and cleanly, with the task of publicly declaring its position and function in the world, a task which was set out and pursued in this document.

An Outing to the Bruderholz

On 15 July 1963 Karl Barth received eighty members of the Württemberg Church Fraternity in Basle, and the following report of the discussion that ensued was prepared by the Rev. W. Schlenker on the basis of a tape-recording.

' "What came ye out for to see?" ' said Karl Barth, when the visitors had settled 'at his feet'. ' "What came ye out for to see?" An old gentleman who has by far the greater part of his life and certainly of his productive life behind him, and is now in retirement?' It soon became plain, however, that this retirement was a very active one. His theological thinking and refreshing humour knew no retirement. Seeing the poise and freedom, the humour and vision, the humility and modesty, with which theology was practised here was an unforgettable experience.

The following question was submitted: 'Professor Barth, you played an important part at the time in the drafting of the Barmen Declaration, Article V of which states: "Scripture tells us that by divine dispensation it is the task of the State in the still unredeemed world in which the Church also lives to provide for justice and peace according to the best of human insight and human ability by the threat or use of force. In gratitude and reverence to God the Church acknowledges the benevolence of this dispensation. The Church reminds men of the kingdom of God, of God's commandment and his righteousness, and hence of the responsibility of rulers and ruled. It trusts and obeys the power of the Word through which God upholds all things."

'Do you still accept this article today, if not its wording, at any rate its substance? If the answer is no, why not? If it is yes, in what way?'

Professor Barth: ' "You played an important part at the time in the drafting of the Barmen Declaration." Yes, that can certainly be said of me. If I remember rightly, Article V was drafted word for word by me, so I must accept responsibility for it. It seems appropriate therefore that I should comment briefly on the details of the wording and explain what was meant by them at the time.

'It begins with the words: "Scripture tells us . . ." It was important at the time to say what had to be said about the State. We do not have a free hand in this matter, but are shown the right way by Holy Scripture, by the testimony of the Old and New Testaments, and Scripture must be understood as referring, not just to individual biblical texts such as Romans 13 (which of course is relevant), but to the whole testimony of the Bible to God's *basileia*, his royal dominion, which has its worldly, human counterpart in the State.

'Now, the article says that "by divine dispensation it is the task of the State . . ." The term " dispensation" was very consciously chosen. The article does not say, for instance, that the State is a divine order. The term "order" was a highly controversial one at the time, for it came very close to the idea of "orders of creation" and others of the same kind.

' "Dispensation" in Latin is *ordinatio*, as distinct from *ordo*, and the meaning here is that the existence of the State as a phenomenon in human history is God-ordained, that it is not, so to speak, purely a product of human nature. In practice God willed and ordained that there should be States.

'The article goes on to speak of the task of the State "to provide for justice and peace". The aim and purpose of the State is thus indicated. Justice and peace represent what can be done in accordance with the divine dispensation for the preservation of man's outward existence. The State is responsible for this, and this, then, is its task.

' "In the still unredeemed world in which the Church also lives". This refers to the fact that the State belongs to a sphere bounded on the one hand by God's already performed act or the sum total of his acts for man's redemption, and on the other hand by the still outstanding revelation of what God has done in the establishment of the covenant. God ordained that the State should be part of the world the reconciliation of which has already taken place though it is not yet apparent.

'The Church also belongs to this world. True, it has a promise which goes beyond the end of all things, the ultimate aim of history, but it must not be forgotten that according to Revelation 21 there will be no temple in the heavenly Jerusalem. All our activities, our preaching and instruction, our church law and our church politics — all this, thank God, will lie behind us, together with a great many other things. In other words the meaning of the Church's activity in the still unredeemed world will have become plain. Judgment will then be delivered, the judgment of a merciful God.

' "According to the best of human insight and human ability". These words are a reminder that the State, though a divine institution, is an institution in the human sphere. It has to be worked by men, men of limited insight and limited abilities. Divine things cannot be expected either from the State or from the Church. The State too can only, as Romans 13 puts it, be a *diakonos* or *leiturgos*, a witness. Divine acts are not performed through the State.

'The article goes on to mention the characteristic feature of the State. I would not say that it was an essential feature, but objectively and in practice the "threat or use of force" is inevitable. The difference between the Church and the State is that in the case of the latter the possibility of the use of force lies in the background, even if in practice it sometimes steps into the foreground.

' "In gratitude and reverence to God the Church acknowledges the benevolence of this dispensation". From the Church's viewpoint, the existence and activity of the State is not to be regarded as a *brutum factum*, a mere fact, let alone an evil. Within the context of the divine dispensation the State has a function which Christians must thankfully and reverently recognize as beneficient. The State belongs to the sphere referred to in the hymn when it says: "What the Lord has created he will maintain." This is rather passive, but the active follows immediately: "The Church reminds men of the kingdom of God, of God's commandment and his righteousness, and hence of the responsibility of rulers and ruled." The Church must remind the State of the kingdom of God, for that is the ultimate, all-embracing reality. It must remind the State that the true kingdom, the kingdom without end, is the kingdom of God, which is founded in Christ, which is already present in the Holy Spirit and will become visible as such in its coming revelation.

'The Church must also remind the State of God's commandment and righteousness, which are of a higher order than the State's. The Church must show the State that it is this higher order that gives meaning to the existence of the State, and so must remind rulers and ruled of their responsibility.

'Thus there is responsibility, or a duty of obedience, not only on the part of the ruled, the so-called subjects of the State. There is also responsibility on the part of the rulers. It is a joint responsibility. Those in whose hands the life of the State is placed are not merely highly placed authorities. Those led or administered by them share the responsibility for the life of the State, its reality and what it is, both in good and evil.

'The Church "trusts and obeys the power of the Word through which God upholds all things". This is a timid reference to what later came to be known as the Christo-

AN OUTING TO THE BRUDERHOLZ

logical foundation of the State. It is an allusion to Hebrews 1:3, "He reflects the glory of God and bears the very stamp of his nature, upholding the universe by his word of power...". That word is Christ. This concluding phrase, without directly mentioning the name of Christ, was intended to indicate that, if the Church recognizes the State, if it acknowledges that in accordance with the injunction of the Scriptures a State there must be, and if it then acts in accordance with its function in relation to the State and reminds it of the kingdom of God, his commandments and righteousness, and summons it to responsibility – if it does all this, it does so with a certain confidence and in a definite spirit of obedience that relies, not on individual texts, but on the power of the Word that is the content of Holy Scripture, the Word that became flesh, through which God upholds all things.

'In the decades since Barmen too little attention has been paid to this Christological justification of the State. Not everyone has noticed what it really says and what was the central point for me when I wrote it.

'So much, then, as a first paraphrase of Article V. And now you put the question to me: "Do you still accept this article today, if not its wording, at any rate its substance? If the answer is no, why not? And if yes, in what way?"

'Yes, in a way I do not think it so bad. In writing it, of course, I had Romans 13 continually in mind. So you can regard it as an attempt to paraphrase Romans 13.

'It was justifiable in the situation at the time. It was drafted in 1934, and all sorts of people took joint responsibility for it. This was just before 30 June 1934.* Nazism was then in its early stages. In 1933 it had behaved quite well. In 1934 it began to bare its claws and things began to get uncomfortable. Many who had gone over to the German Christians remorsefully left them again. And some

---

* The date of the bloody suppression by Hitler of the so-called Röhm *Putsch*.

people in the Church began to realize that something ought to be done. And so these various synods were held. If you bear in mind that these words were written in the world of Hitler, Göring and Goebbels, and whatever the rest of them were called, it can be claimed that at least it was made very clear that the attitude of Christianity to the State was rather different from that trumpeted abroad by the Nazis. If at least all Christians – to say nothing of the others – had listened to Article V, German history might perhaps have been different.

'But God willed otherwise, and that perhaps entitles one to say that it was not good enough. Perhaps a good deal of it should have been put quite differently.

'It should also be borne in mind that we drafted it under pressure. It had to be as brief as possible. We could not discuss the whole theology of the State or the Christian's attitude to the State. We had to say something right in ten lines. Brevity is the soul of wit, but of course it has its obscurities, so that questions naturally arise out of some of those statements.

'Nowadays I should probably put some things differently, but I shall return to that later. Now I should like to ask what your criticisms are. What strictures on Article V of the Barmen Declaration are in the air?'

Herr Schlenker, wishing to express the desire of the fraternity for an unequivocal stand for peace on the part of the Church, said it was satisfactory that the article did not put forward a metaphysics of the State, did not discuss the value or nature of the State, but simply stated its task.

Yet the question still arose whether it was the God-ordained duty of the State to provide for justice and peace by the threat or use of force. The question arose whether it was a Christian duty to participate in the threat or use of force. The New Testament nowhere mentioned that Christians should in any way be involved in the threat or use of force by the State authorities. That could not be concluded from Romans 13. Was it right to justify and sanction the use of force by the State in Article V? They should remind the State that its essential function was to provide for justice and peace. But Christians could best provide this service to the State by refusing to participate in the use of arms. The State was in any case exposed to the temptation of the premature use of force and thus to the misuse of its power, and it was only by refusing to use arms that Christians could point to the State's primary duty of preserving life.

Herr Weitbrecht referred to Nebuchadnezzar who, according to Romans 13, had to serve God's plan of redemption whether he wanted to or not. Political authority was an instrument with which God carried out his plan. But the situation of Christians was different, for it was also their duty within the ordinances of the State to seek the best, and they were directly addressed by God and were directly subject to him. The State somehow functioned on the left hand of God.

Herr Schlenker mentioned an interview in which Professor Barth had said, in reply to a question, that if he had not been a theologian he might have become a traffic policeman. The service the traffic policeman performed was very plain; his work was meaningful, necessary and salutary. What they were now concerned with was the difference between the meaningful work of the traffic police and the actions of those who used force and shed blood, because the latter immediately put a question mark against the Christian testimony of God's love and reconciliation with all mankind. Their chief criticism of Article V was that it could too easily be used to justify the misuse of force by the State.

Herr Rücker said: 'You told us earlier with satisfaction, Professor, that even Mahraens and Meister accepted Barmen, Article V.'

'And you should have seen their embarrassment when they

got up', Professor Barth interjected. 'I can still see their faces now.'

Herr Rücker went on to say that all he meant was that their problem today was that when they opposed nuclear armament their critics turned on them and said: 'But look, here in the Barmen Declaration is theological authority for the State's use of force or the threat of force, which is divinely ordained.' Those who accepted nuclear rearmament asked whether they still held to Barmen V now that they repudiated this form of the use or threat of force by the State.

Herr Mack said that the Bible spoke essentially of persons, of kings and potentates, while Barmen V spoke of institutions. Did that not make a difference? The Bible dealt with individuals, while they had deviated in the direction of metaphysics, so that they saw nothing but institutions.

Herr Poguntke asked whether it might not help to clarify the matter if the wording were changed to read: 'The duty of the State is, to the best of human insight, ... to provide for justice and peace, even to the point of making use of the threat or the exercise of force.' This would mean that the State's use of force was divinely permitted and accepted, but that the task of Christianity and the Church was clearly marked off from this sphere, and it would be clear that the threat or exercise of force was no part of the Church's or the Christian's duty.

Professor Barth said his reply would bring him to what he himself would now question in Article V. 'You suggested a phrase such as "even to the point of ...",' he continued. 'I would say "if necessary by the threat or use of force". I still cannot see how this can be omitted completely. I should most certainly object if it were said that the essential characteristic of the State was the use of force; the State may use force only as a last resource. If we tried to leave it out completely, there would be no more State to talk about. Even the traffic policeman carries a pistol, or at any rate a truncheon. The State does not use only friendly persuasion in providing for peace and justice. Policemen should always be friendly and polite, but friendliness unfortunately has its limits. The question is simply whether force can be eliminated. In my *Church Dogmatics* I said that force is part, not of the *opus proprium* (real work) of the State, but of its *opus alienum* (strange work). The use of force is a last resource.

'Earlier a questioner said in effect: "What have we Christians to do with these questions? The New Testament does not expect Christians to involve themselves in the use of force by the State."

'Well, Christians are at all events expected to pray for kings and those in authority. I reached my whole position in the matter when I said to myself: When I really pray, I cannot remain totally inactive myself. When I pray, I make myself responsible for those in authority. From that it is but a small step to admitting that I myself am a person in authority. All this is not something that merely concerns others, but *tua res agitur*. And hence the idea of the responsibility of rulers and ruled.

'Is that a justification of the use of force? If you reproach me with what certain people in Germany say to you about Article V, are they not obviously misusing it? The article is not a justification of the use of force. If its whole point is sought in the parenthetical remark about "the threat or use of force" it is completely misunderstood.

'It is concerned with the establishment of justice and peace. That is the State's task, and that is what Article V affirms. The justification of the State is that there is a divine dispensation to this end, which unfortunately cannot be carried out totally and cleanly without the use of truncheons and other still more dangerous instruments.

'The work of Christians in the world may include responsible involvement in using or threatening force. Whether it is right or wrong in particular cases is of course open to discussion.

'The use of force is of course the State's problem. It does not begin only when the bullets start flying, but is involved in imposing fines, raising taxes and locking up people for their own and society's good.

'Today I should not merely say that the duty of the State is to provide for justice and peace. I should amplify this and say that the State must serve the common good and thus provide for justice, peace and freedom. (The fine idea of freedom was missing in 1934.)

'What matters is the common good of humanity, and I must say I approve of the term used by Pope John XXIII. The State must serve the common good on the basis of freedom. So no compulsory welfare measures, then. And in that case of course the words "if necessary by the threat or use of force" could be added.

'I do not much like the mention of the kingdom of God, God's commandment and his righteousness in the same line. The kingdom of God is an all-embracing idea. I should say that the Church proclaims the kingdom of God (i.e. Jesus Christ, who came and will come again, that is, Jesus Christ as the Kyrios), and hence God's righteousness (in the biblical sense of the term, in that he works righteousness, the righteousness of his mercy, the righteousness of his love). And only from there should I go on to mention God's commandment. In other words, I should begin with the eschatological idea of the kingdom of God and then state its practical content, God's righteousness in the forgiveness of sins. That is the purport of the Old and New Testaments: the *dikaiosyne theou* (the righteousness of God) and not some other kind of "justice".

'God's commandment follows from this. The Gospel and the law. The duty of the Church in the State, in relation to the State, is to approve or to repudiate the State as it is in actual practice. Thus I should put it as follows:

AN OUTING TO THE BRUDERHOLZ

The Church proclaims the kingdom of God, his righteousness and commandment. It reminds Christians and non-Christians of their political responsibility. By this I mean that Christians – it is they themselves and not others. who are the State – must pray for the State, but also work for it. The principle of the link between prayer and work, *ora et labora*, should be demonstrated and carried out.'

The following question was also put to Professor Barth: 'The statements in your *Church Dogmatics*, Volume III, Part Four, pp. 460 ff., are gladly quoted by many who approve of the political path being followed by the German Federal Government to the point of calling for nuclear rearmament and willingness to accept nuclear warfare. Do you still stand by those statements, and, if so, on what grounds?'

Professor Barth replied: 'I have once more read through, not just pp. 460 ff., but the whole context on the problem of war in the *Church Dogmatics*.

'All that was written in 1951. And while reading through it – as often happens to me when reading my own work – my first impression was that it was not at all bad, that there was a good deal in it that was worth reading; and I cannot entirely reject it even today. All the same, I should say that it is perhaps not one of the happiest parts of the *Church Dogmatics*. That is connected with the fact that it is so closely linked with practical matters. For it is very easy for the landscape so to change in the course of thirteen years that in retrospect one wishes that one had put certain things differently. But, in the first place, what I said was ninety-nine per cent anti-war. I hope that made an impression on you. I have been told that my denunciation of war was among the most effective that have been made. I certainly cannot be accused of being a war theologian. On the other hand, the case I made is not pacifism. But I pointed out that the whole development of the war question shows that war must be excluded. We no longer have the *naïveté* towards the soldier that Luther could still have. We know too much about how wars arise and their real motives. Nowadays war is a matter that concerns all mankind. It has become so terrible that the question arises ever more acutely whether it is still tolerable, whether it is still possible for a nation to be in a situation so desperate as to justify it in saying that it must fight.

'When I wrote the *Dogmatics*, I considered that war could still be justifiable, that it might be the necessary price to pay for the necessary preservation of a State. And in such extreme cases, which constitute the one per cent, it would be possible to speak of the just and necessary war in which Christians would have to join.

'Now, if someone comes along and says that Karl Barth says that war is defensible, that there is such a thing as the *bellum justum*, the just war, and if people actually get up in the German Bundestag with the *Dogmatics* in their hand and quote it to justify war, that is of course sheer wickedness. When they do that, of course, the three and a half lines in small print in which I said I would fight for Switzerland are immensely important. Even President Heuss quoted them, and said: "So what applies south of Lörrach does not apply north of it? Therefore Germany must rearm." All I can say to that is that it is sheer dishonesty. It must be borne in mind that we had just emerged from Hitler's war. So far as I myself was concerned, I was determined that Hitler must never enter Switzerland. If those three and a half lines are now dwelt on and used as an argument for the just war, it is sheer malevolence. That is not the way to quote. Anyone who has read that chapter honestly will notice that I added with my last breath, as it were, that perhaps it will have to happen all over again. Yet there are theologians and others who say: Look, he has admitted that there is such a thing as a just war, and the jubilation begins.

'But that is not really the dreadful thing that I now regret. What I now regret is the absence of the point made in the encyclical *Pacem in terris*, namely that "in our age that prides itself on being the atomic age it is contrary to reason to regard war as a suitable means of restoring rights that have been infringed on".

'That is the point that I did not take into account. Five or six years had passed since Hiroshima. I should have realized and said that the appearance of atomic weapons had so changed the situation that one must say: This is enough. What I said about war in that one per cent could still be said if the implications of nuclear warfare were excluded. War has never been a fine thing. Even the Battle of Sempach was not a fine thing. But again and again it is argued that if it must be, it must be. But there is a fallacy in that logic. Nuclear warfare from the outset means the end of all things. It makes waging war senseless. And that is the point that is missing from my book. In connection with the idea of the just war, I should have said that, in considering the question of whether a war is just or not, not only its cause and meaning must be taken into account, but also the manner of its waging. Had I done that, I should have been bound to conclude that no nuclear war can be a just war. Such a war can be nothing but unjust, and the Christian can have no alternative but to refuse it.'

Herr Rücker said he was worried by one passage in the *Church Dogmatics*: ' "There may well be bound up with the independent life of a nation responsibility for the whole physical, intellectual and spiritual life of the people comprising it, and therefore their relationship to God. It may well be that in and with the independence of a nation there is entrusted to its people something which . . . they may not therefore surrender" [cf. Volume III, Part Four, p. 462]. That is your justification of war as a last recourse, the one per cent. Can this passage not be used as justification for the idea of an anti-Communist crusade? In Württemberg the argument that Communism is spiritual murder is used by anti-Communist campaigners.'

Professor Barth replied: 'By "threat to the spiritual relationship to God" I meant something other than the threat to religious instruction in schools and things of that sort. I was merely thinking very concretely of what would have happened if we in Switzerland had given in to Hitler. There were enough people in Switzerland who wanted to give in, who said in the summer of 1940 for instance: "Let us fit ourselves into the new Europe; who knows, perhaps a new age is dawning."

'It was clear to me that this was no longer merely a political matter. This was sheer wickedness, something that simply must not be allowed to happen. It would mean denying a gift of God and trampling it underfoot. Therefore it had to be resisted. But that had nothing to do with Communist propaganda for atheism or an anti-Communist crusade, but simply with a situation in which I was existentially involved, in which it was clear to me that we were faced with something that in no circumstances could be allowed to happen. I wrote that passage with such a situation in mind.'

Herr Dieterich: 'But that is how many people feel who have looked at the Berlin wall or have been in East Germany. They too say, out of existential experience, that this is something to which they can only say one hundred per cent no.'

Professor Barth: 'Well, one should reason with such people – about the wall, and the relations between the German Federal Republic and the German Democratic Republic. Also the situation is different, for now the atomic bomb is involved. I would not say now that Switzerland must be defended with the atomic bomb. That would be lunacy. It cannot be done. It would mean destroying what I want to defend.'

The following question was submitted to Professor Barth: 'In the exercise of our ecclesiastical duties the problem of baptism and confirmation is becoming more and more acute. Some brothers believe that it can be solved only if infant baptism is accompanied by instruction of the parents. Others believe that, since the meaning of baptism has been obscured to the point of unrecognizability by the practice of infant baptism, the Church should in principle return to adult baptism. Thirdly, there are brothers who believe that the evil can be overcome in the long run by the postponement of confirmation to a later stage and devising a completely different type of instruction for confirmation candidates. What advice can you give us?'

Professor Barth said: 'In reply to this question I would say that I agree in principle with the second group of brothers who believe that "since the meaning of baptism has been obscured to the point of unrecognizability by the practice of infant baptism, the Church should in principle return to adult baptism". It says here "the Church should in principle return to adult baptism". I do not like the term "adult baptism". The point at issue here is that of responsibility, both that of the baptizing congregation and that of the future Christian who is to be baptized. The point is that the congregation should not simply say: Here is a couple who have a child. The couple belong to the congregation, so the child belongs to it too. The child is not asked, and the whole question of responsibility is put aside. That will not do.

'Everything that we read about baptism in the New Testament, from the baptism in the Jordan by John to the various baptisms in the Acts, makes it plain that both the baptizers and the baptized knew what they were about. The baptizers did not just go ahead and baptize, and the baptized did not let it take place without attempting to understand its meaning. Instead, questions were asked, the Gospel was preached, people were present who believed, and said: "What prevents me from being baptized?" And then they were baptized.

This state of affairs seems to me to be the only possible one if baptism is not to decay through further centuries. The point is not whether the person to be baptized is an adult or is aged ten or twelve, but that he should want to be baptized, should say of his own accord: "I believe, and want to belong to the congregation", and that the congregation should acknowledge this and thereupon baptize him, and that the joint action should take place on a basis of freedom of thought and action. We must escape from this dark and gloomy atmosphere in which no one really knows what is really happening. The godchild does not know, neither do the parents and the godparents, nor does the congregation that sits there and sings hymns Something is done in a – I do not want to say mystical – but certainly a semi-magical frame of mind, and then "Suffer the little children to come unto me" is read, though it has nothing to do with baptism, and the famous text from Acts 2, "the promise is to you and to your children", though that has nothing to do with baptism either. And so it goes on, and the Church is watered down, literally watered down with holy water, and then men complain about the dismal state of the churches, which people belong to though they have no faith. But why should that be expected of the poor wretches, since they were never consulted when they were brought or carried into this assembly, dressed in white, with a godmother standing here and a godfather standing there and a good meal afterwards, and the minister who so amiably bends over the infant and sprinkles it with water? It's all very fine, but basically – and this applies not only to the Catholics but also to us Lutherans and Calvinists – what we perform here is an act of antiquated magic. Baptism must be removed from that atmosphere. That is why I agree with the brothers who want to give up infant baptism.

'Primarily, of course, all this is a question of exegesis. I can only offer my own exegesis, and invite people to read the New Testament. Where in the New Testament will they find any guidance pointing to baptism as we practise it today?

'Of course I cannot lay down the law here either, but I appeal to Scripture and to those who read and respect it and abide by it. It is there that real discussion of baptism begins, not that dreadful kind of endless discussion of the subject that always boils down to the fact that people simply want infant baptism and one does not sufficiently realize that it is a custom many centuries old. Hardly any custom or tradition is so deep-seated.

'In Württemberg – to say nothing of Switzerland – you can be a wicked heretic in regard to the Holy Trinity. You can be a Sabellian, or an Arian, or what you will. You can take what liberties you like with the Chalcedonian Creed. You can demythologize and existentialize. But one thing you cannot do. You cannot oppose infant baptism, for it is far too deep-seated. Have you ever heard a protest against infant baptism from the Bultmann school? They would not dream of it. They demythologize everything; but not that. Why not? Because it is more deep-seated than the Resurrection. It is in fact no problem at all, because the resurrection of Christ requires the Holy Spirit and faith, while the institution of infant baptism simply exists, more solidly than the Berlin wall, or Cologne Cathedral, or what you will. It is simply part of the landscape. The mere idea of doing away with it or even putting a question mark against it calls almost for the courage of a hero.'

Professor Barth was asked: 'To what extent are the sacraments and the so-called ministerial offices proclamation and therefore unconditionally to be offered, applied and granted to all? To what extent, therefore, are they a form and a law to which the believer's obedience should be demanded and secured? Do the proper administration of the sacraments and the legitimate ministerial offices burst the bounds of established church forms?'

Professor Barth replied: 'I should like to say something about the second part of your question, because I am not in entire agreement with the way in which it is put. I should say rather: "To what extent are the sacraments and the so-called ministerial offices proclamation and therefore unconditionally to be offered, applied and granted to all, and to what extent are they part of the believer's response and of the application of faith . . . ?"

'To that I would answer that the sacraments are nothing whatever but response, the response not only of the candidate for baptism but also of the congregation. What takes place in baptism, communion and proclamation is all response. There are these remarkable relics (I said something about them this morning when I mentioned *praedicatio verbi divini est verbum divinum*) of the idea that by our own actions – whether in proclamation or in the sacraments – we could, as it were, set the divine allocution in motion. That is something we are totally unable to do. All we can do is witness how God speaks. Witness, however, is response. The whole life of the Church from top to bottom is nothing but response to the Word of God. The Church lives under the promise and the hope that in this response, this echo to God's Word (whether in the form of preaching, the sacraments, or religious instruction), God's Word itself will become audible.

'It is not our task, so to speak, to produce this echo. Nor can we do so, for it is beyond us. Our modest task is response.

'And to that I would add that the whole matter of the sacraments – when I am talking seriously I do not like the term sacraments, which has so remarkably permeated the

Christian vocabulary – this whole subject can be restored to health again only when we have become clear in our minds that the beginning and the end, the alpha and the omega, of the congregation, the individuals who join it and the individuals who live in it, is response. We do so in the promise that "where two or three are gathered in my name, there am I in the midst of them". The congregation abides by the promise that "there am I in the midst of them". I, the Lord. Everything depends on their thinking strictly of him, looking to him, witnessing to him, honouring him.

'The words "I baptize you in the name of the Father and the Son and the Holy Spirit" are spoken in this sense. In the name of what is revealed in the Bible. So, what is said is something like this: "I now tell you of God's revelation. I tell you this, believing in the Father, the Son and the Holy Spirit".

'But this is a witnessing. The hearer can hear it and accept it as a promise. His acceptance itself is a response. A response, not to the minister's words, but to God's, which both the minister and the person being baptized have now heard.

'And at Holy Communion the words "This is my body and my blood" are spoken. What is this but the gathering of Christians to eat and drink together at his invitation, the crowning moment of the Christian service of worship, this act of eating and drinking together that is not just being together but is being in communion; "this is my body and my blood"?

'It is a matter, not of emptying baptism and communion of their content, but of filling them with their right content, and doing so by looking at the actions of the congregation and of individual Christians.

'At this time I would not put so much emphasis on faith. I have not used that word here, because so much mischief is done with it nowadays. The most dreadful things are done with it. Of course faith plays its part in the sacraments, but I would put the whole emphasis on the action of the congregation and of individual Christians, that is, action in the Word and of course action in faith, love and hope. This action is response, and if it has the promise it is no empty matter, and it is not merely a matter of symbols, but of reality, and not a semi-divine or fully divine reality, but the reality that falls to the Church. For at this point darkness always keeps falling when we try to play God, whether in the pulpit or at the communion table or at the font. Our business is not to play God, but to respond and obey as men who have been called. This obedience is the reality of the life of the Church.

'It is vital that it should be realized that there is One who calls, One whom we have to obey and respond to.

'That is why I am so delighted at Helmut Gollwitzer's book *The Existence of God in the Confession of Faith*, because he has worked this out in reply to those people. We are continually told that we must get rid of the subject-object relationship. Nonsense! The subject-object relationship is not the issue. The issue is the encounter of God and men, God's existence and reality in his speech and action. I am not angry with the Korahites because of their demythologizing, but because they try to eliminate the subject, the person of God, *dei loquentis persona*, as Calvin put it, so that the person of God evaporates and merges into faith, and we end by being asked to have faith in our faith. That is arrant nonsense.

'Now I have come to these questions myself, but they are relevant to the sacraments and proclamation. It is important to view the sacraments and proclamation together, because we have someone over against us: "Behold, I am among them." *I*, not any kind of hypostatsis of faith.'

Herr Röhm expressed gratitude to Professor Barth for what he had said to them about baptism, and said he would like to draw attention to the statement on the subject made by the Tübingen faculty in 1950, which contained propositions that could have appeared in the *Church Dogmatics*, though the theologians who drafted it were mostly of the Marburg school. There were some young ministers in Württemberg who did want their children to be baptized in infancy. They included members of the Marburg as well as of the Basle school. It was gratifying that there was a common approach to the question of baptism among members of both schools.

Professor Barth: 'There is something I should like to add in regard to this practical question, namely that there are ministers who do not have their own children baptized in infancy. I once had two visitors in a fortnight. The first was a minister who did not want to have his child baptized, and the second was his superior, who complained bitterly about his unwillingness to abide by the regulations. He asked me what might happen, and seemed pretty determined to dismiss the man. I find this severity alarming.

'I have had this problem in my own family. One of my sons – also a theologian – had his first two children baptized. Meanwhile his theological development continued. When his third child arrived, he said to me: "Things can't go on like this. You are against infant baptism, and so are my wife and I. Things can't go on like this." So the third child was not baptized.

'The question arises whether this is the right way. It could be suggested that it might be better not to introduce a new order in the minister's house, but to wait for the congregation, to set about patiently instructing it, in spite of the possibility that one might fail. But patient instruction of the congregation must begin somewhere. It must be instructed on the basis that I tried to indicate previously, so that this tremendously strong tradition may be slowly undermined and eventually the question of whether infant baptism can be allowed to go on like this may come from the congregation itself.

'The minister's example does not help very much. That was the case in my son's parish. He took the matter of baptismal instruction very seriously, of course, and interviewed both parents. He said to them: "It is a church regulation that the child should be baptized. I shall baptize it if that is your wish. But I should like you to consider whether it might not be better to wait till it is older." However, the success of these efforts was not very impressive. A tradition as strong as this cannot of course be overthrown in a few years.

'That does not of course mean that everything should remain as it is. "Do not quench the spirit", I called down the steps after the young minister's superior when he left me, for I really had the feeling that he wanted to do just that. If anyone should want to quench the spirit that moves one or other of you, you must defend yourselves, stand by your cause, but perhaps not too militantly. I have mentioned this incident only because earlier we were talking about ministers who did not want their own children baptized in infancy. I am delighted that serious doubts about the matter have been raised at Marburg. I see from current literature that demythologizing goes briskly on, but I have never seen anything about baptism yet in *Kerygma and Myth*.'

Herr Rücker: 'Would you say that we should restrict ourselves to applying to our governing bodies for a change in the regulations that would give us greater freedom of action in this respect?'

Professor Barth: 'Yes, that is something one might well do. There are already whole churches, in France, for instance, in which there is at least the possibility of choice between infant baptism and baptism at a responsible age. But you will find that, even if the regulations allow that degree of freedom, the change will not come about so quickly. But at any rate the door would be open.

'If I were the governing body of the Church and favoured

infant baptism, I think I should be a trifle Mephistophelian or Machiavellian and say: Yes, we shall grant you this. You'll see that you won't get very far with it. It is possible that many members of these church councils secretly think in that way. For the real obstacle is not church regulations but congregational tradition, opposing which will for a long time to come be like knocking one's head against a brick wall.'

Herr Gugel: 'If someone comes to the minister and says "I want my child to be baptized, but of course my wife and I regard all that stuff you tell us about God and Christ as a lot of moonshine", what is the minister to do?'

Professor Barth: 'That would be obvious fraud, of course. I should simply say no, the child will not be baptized. If the parents actually say it is a lot of moonshine, even the infant baptism regulations say that that is the extreme case in which it should be refused. But it cannot occur so dreadfully often. There are few who come out so frankly with such admissions. There are many who think them in secret. But in that situation I should say no, the child will not be baptized. That is no punishment. The parents should be told: "You want the child baptized only because it is the custom. You have no serious intention, no faith, so drop it. Let us wait and see how the child develops." It does not follow that children from such unchurchly families will not later find their way to the congregation.

'On the basis of things as they now stand, perhaps one should not question parents too vigorously. Poor creatures of that kind cannot be expected suddenly to become believing parents. Perhaps it may become possible to expect that of them at a later stage. These are not the circumstances in which too deep an examination of conscience should be carried out.'

Professor Barth brought the discussion to an end by expressing the pleasure the gathering had given him. He had spent more than forty years thinking about these questions, and had travelled a long way since the publication of the *Epistle to the Romans* in 1919. In this discussion he had spoken mainly off the cuff. He had talked freely rather than dogmatically. He would be delighted if anything he had said had been helpful to anyone.

A Thank-You and a Bow
—Kierkegaard's Reveille

Speech on being awarded the Sonning Prize

Can you imagine the feelings – the surprise, the bewilderment – of one who unexpectedly one morning receives from a far country the news that he has been awarded a prize the previous recipients of which include such illustrious names as Winston Churchill, Albert Schweitzer, Igor Stravinsky and Niels Bohr, and that the reason given for the award is his great contribution to European culture? Is Saul also among the prophets? How shall I make out in the company of these men? That was my first startled reaction.

My second reaction, and the question arising out of it, were of a somewhat different nature. The news had come from Denmark, from Copenhagen; that is, from the city on whose streets – beloved by a few, feared or ridiculed by a few, but unknown to many – there once walked Søren Kierkegaard. What if I should meet him here? And what if he should accost me with words like these, continuing certain pointed discourses that he addressed to the theologians of his time? 'So this is how things are with you, my dear friend, at the end of your theological and other life. This – gallant witness to the truth! – is what you have come to after the stormy irruption of your *Epistle to the Romans*, after all those more or less disturbing journals and polemical treatises of yours, and the many volumes of your non-conforming *Church Dogmatics*. So you have come to the point at which they offer you a State prize – and that on the basis of merits that are somewhat curious from the Christian point of view. My belief was that you might deserve a measure of praise as a little genius, though by my standards something might be said even about that. But as an apostle? Apostles, if I remember rightly, were not awarded prizes, they were rather – you know what I mean.' I was afraid that I might meet the shadow of this man in Copenhagen, and that he would speak to me today in that fashion.

My third reaction after receiving the news was of yet another kind. This I can express in a form other than the interrogative. I had, and still have, cause to be purely and simply grateful that your university thought of me of all people for the award of a Sonning Prize. Thank-you in Greek is *eucharistia*. Thanks are a response to a constituent of that Greek word; they are the response to *charis*, that is, to a freely given gift of an undeserved good. Thanks are the disposition towards and the action *vis-à-vis* that which one has not sought, has not expected, does not claim, but simply receives. The news from the far north evoked this kind of thanks in me, and I wish to express them in that sense to you, honourable Rector and honourable colleagues of the University of Copenhagen. Such a prize cannot be earned. One can receive it only in amazement. One can respond to it only with pure gratitude.

I should like, however, to be permitted to add that I feel and express this gratitude not least as a representative of the entire theological guild. If I correctly interpret my selection as recipient of the Sonning Prize, it implies the recognition that to a right European culture there belong, not only a right science, art, and politics, but also a right theology – perhaps not least a right theology. What we might call European culture was once to a large extent the product of a theological environment. Whether this culture will emerge from the crisis into which it has passed in our century will once again depend on whether the first and last question – which is precisely the question of theology – is alive and finds a right answer. Right theology is today, as

A THANK-YOU AND A BOW

at all times, a matter of difficult, uphill and, in the eyes of most people, scarcely impressive work. Thus many of those who do this work will be encouraged as I am, and grateful as I am, that you were willing on this occasion to consider a choice against which much might have been said, that is, the choice of a theologian.

It has been intimated to me that, in addition to this word of thanks, I might, within the brevity suggested by the scope of this occasion, say something pertinent to my particular theological work. What could be more *à propos* in Copenhagen than briefly to outline the story of my relations with the celebrated Dane whom I have already mentioned and made speak to us—so that at this hour that wholesome intruder Søren Kierkegaard might not be absent?

The first book of his I ever bought was *The Instant*, and that was in 1909. I assume that I also read it at that time. But it cannot have made a deep impression on me then, as I was very much occupied with and energetically set on the theology of Harnack, Herrmann, and the *Christliche Welt*. Because I was preoccupied with other things during the following years, especially with Socialism, Kierkegaard had a respite from me—and I from him. He entered my thinking to a more serious and greater extent only in about 1919, at a critical juncture between the first and second editions of my *Epistle to the Romans*, and from that time onwards he played an important role in my writing. By 1916 a number of us of the younger generation had hesitantly set out to introduce a theology better than that of the nineteenth century and of the turn of the century—better in the sense that in it God, in his unique position over against man, and especially religious man, might clearly be given that honour we believed we found him to have in the Bible. But the strength and magnitude of the emphasis on God as the basis and object of faith, an emphasis for which Hermann Kutter then provided the stimulation, became plain to us only gradually. The first edition of my *Epistle to the Romans* lacked much in this respect. Among the older authorities whom in the years 1919 and 1920 we thought partly to support our alarms and partly to urge us onwards, in addition to Dostoevsky, the older and younger Blumhardts, the odd stranger Overbeck and the great Plato – yes, you heard correctly, Plato – there was also this Søren Kierkegaard; the reformers of the sixteenth century did not yet evoke much response in us. What attracted us particularly to him, what we rejoiced in, and what we learned, was the criticism, so unrelenting in its incisiveness, with which he attacked so much: all the speculation that blurred the infinite qualitative difference between God and man, all the aesthetic playing down of the absolute claims of the Gospel and of the necessity to do it justice by personal decision; in short, all the attempts to make the scriptural message innocuous, all the excessively pretentious and at the same time excessively cheap Christianism and churchiness of prevalent theology from which we ourselves were not yet quite free. In the second phase of the revolution in which we were then involved he became one of the cocks whose crowing seemed to proclaim from near and far the dawn of a really new day. The second edition of my *Epistle to the Romans* is the very telling document of my participation in what has been called 'the Kierkegaard Renaissance'. There were to be for all of us, and indeed especially for me, new dawns with new questions and answers, and yet I believe that throughout my theological life I have remained faithful to Kierkegaard's reveille as we heard it then, and that I am still faithful to it today. Going back to Hegel or even Bishop Mynster has been out of the question ever since.

It is true, however – and this several people have pointed out – that in my later books, writings, and sermons, express references to Kierkegaard have become fewer and fewer. His peculiar sound has not become silent, but has been muted by other sounds and has become a strong accompaniment side by side with others. In fact, by reason of a glad agreement with him in his militant aspect, I had at first overlooked certain features of his historical appearance.

Was it permissible to bring into focus the contrasts, contradictions, and precipices that Kierkegaard had sketched so masterfully? Was it permissible to formulate more strictly still the conditions for thinking and living in faith, in love, and in hope? Was it permissible to make and thus again and again effect the truly necessary *negations* about the subject of theology and thereby to cause the poor wretches who became Christians, or might want to think of themselves as such, to taste again and again the bitterness of the training required? Was that permissible, if the aim was to proclaim and to interpret the Gospel of God and thus the Gospel of his free grace? It is odd how easily one is caught in the wheels of a law that can only deaden and make one sour, gloomy, and sad.

Further, what about the individual in whose existence nearly everything seems to be centred for Kierkegaard? Where in his teaching are the people of God, the congregation, the Church; where are her diaconal and missionary charge, her political and social charge? What does it mean that, in interpreting the command 'Thou shalt love thy neighbour as thyself', Kierkegaard could agree with St Augustine and Scholasticism against Luther and Calvin that there must be a love of self that takes precedence over love of others? How strange that we, who were just coming from an intense preoccupation with the relation of Christianity to the social question, did not immediately become suspicious at the point of Kierkegaard's pronounced holy individualism.

Thirdly, did not a new anthropocentric system announce itself in Kierkegaard's theoretical groundwork – one quite opposed to that at which we aimed? The fact that the existential philosophy of Heidegger, Jaspers, and Sartre could grow out of and be based on his work is understandable and legitimate, on the proviso that Kierkegaard wanted to be and was a Christian thinker in his own way. But a theology oriented decisively towards and subsisting essentially on Kierkegaard was possible only where Schleiermacher had not been read with sufficient care and one had not been warned definitely against a continuation of his programme, including an existential one. Where this warning was not heard, the experiment with a subjectivity that as such regarded itself as the truth was taken over anew in just this form. It was an experiment with a faith founded in and moved by itself and thus groundless and without object. Under the signature of Kierkegaard's existential dialectic a genuine theological reaction has sprung up in the middle of our century. That such a thing could have been made possible by him is a third consideration that did not enter our minds forty years ago. To sum up, Kierkegaard was bound more closely to the nineteenth century than we were willing to believe at that time. We may perhaps raise the historically pointed question whether his teaching was not itself the highest, most consistent, and most thoroughly reflective completion of pietism, which in the eighteenth century, along with rationalism, laid the foundations of that Christianism and churchiness of the pious that Kierkegaard opposed so passionately and we, forty years ago, set out to oppose anew by invoking his name among our allies. We could not attack its foundation, man-centred Christianity as such, from a Kierkegaardian basis, because he himself had not attacked but rather fortified it immensely.

In the light of these later insights, I am and will remain thankful as before to Kierkegaard for the immunization he gave me in those days. I am and will remain filled with deep respect for the genuinely tragic nature of his life and the extraordinary intellectual brilliance of his work. I consider him to be a teacher whose school every theologian must enter once. Woe to him who misses it – provided only he does not remain in or return to it. Kierkegaard's teaching, as he himself once said, is the seasoning for the food, but not the food itself which it is the task of right theology to offer to the Church and thus to men. Primarily the Gospel is the glad news of God's 'yes' to man. Secondly it is the news that the congregation must pass on to the whole world. Thirdly it is the news from on high. These are three aspects with regard to which, after my encounter with Kierkegaard, I had to do further study in the schools of other teachers.

Kierkegaard and the Theologians

There are theologians who may have heard something about and may also have read something of Kierkegaard but have never passed through his school. They have not had to stand up to him. Somehow they have got by him. Whether their thinking is more orthodox or more liberal, more pietistic or evangelical or social or political, more speculative or more activistic, whether their strength lies in preaching or in teaching, in pastoral care or in learning, these men are characterized by a cheerfulness of speech and conduct that in the long run never fails them. Their vocation as such constitutes no challenge to them. They know 'what is what', and thus are not aware of any embarrassments. They know Christianity and their position as its representatives to be securely fitted into the structure of the other elements and functions of human society. They are glad to see Christianity, and with it their own activity, sanctioned and basically approved by all good men. Among these good men they are not in an alien place, but rather at home as part of them. Apart from occasional harmless disturbances, they are at peace with themselves, with the Church, with the world, and so also with God. So far as they are concerned, Kierkegaard lived, suffered, and struggled in vain.

There are other theologians who have worked themselves deeper and deeper into Kierkegaard, so much so that they could not work themselves out of him again. They are men who thus failed to graduate from the senior year of his school. The infinite qualitative difference between God and man, with all its consequences, has eaten itself right into them. They see themselves and the others, the Church and the world, surrounded by nothing but threatening negations. To them their vocation is a continuous temptation, their genuine, authentic Christianity one continuous attack on all other 'Christianities'. The salvation of human existence is their concern in their ever fresh awareness of its absolute questionableness. Their message is that the vacuum is filled and must be emptied again and again, made clean of what keeps filling it. Their sad pleasure or pleasurable sadness is the irony that they see covering everything, the irony with which they themselves cover everything; it is a seriousness that never allows them to be really serious, a smile that can never be laughter. Even if, in practice, they do not imitate the Master in all things – if, for instance, they not only get engaged but also marry in the usual way – they nevertheless try to make plain, as much as is possible in their conduct and their teaching and perhaps also in their writings and their books, that they seek neither to stand up nor to lie down, but to be in a state of suspension, and that they are annoyed with their environment when it does not itself try to be in that same state. To them Kierkegaard has become a system.

A third kind of theologian has also read Kierkegaard and attended his school – but has passed out of it. These men also experienced alarm on account of him, they too were shaken by the tremendous otherness of his Christianity, the newness of his message and the severity of his demands. The problematical character of human existence uncovered by him alarmed them too. They too could not put behind them the stimulus received from him, and could no longer succumb to the slumber of a merely aesthetical piety. They too could not return to the flesh-pots of a bourgeois Christianism and a churchiness of either ancient or modern coloration, could never again ignore or suppress the 'no', uttered in the Gospel to the world and the Church. But – and this led them beyond Kierkegaard – they could now just hear it and bear witness to it as the 'no' enfolded in God's 'yes'; they could bear witness to it as the fire of his love, which aims, not only at this or that individual, but at the entire godless world and seeks to be proclaimed as such by the Church. Only thus could they understand and give validity precisely to the incisiveness of that 'no'. It lost its philosophical, its axiomatic character. Without thereby becoming silent, the 'no' could no longer be the law imposed on them and others. It could no longer be their theme. Their desperation changed to confident desperation, Luther's *desperatio fiducialis*. Their vocation, and the challenge confronting them in it even now, were subsumed under the sign of hope. They found the comfort of the ever so pitiful Christians, the comfort which is for the whole world and so for them too, in what God, in the majesty of his free grace, has done, is still doing, and will do again and conclusively, for and with man. They sought it there instead of in something that man could be or do on his own for God. Resting on this, they could not interchange theology, secretly or openly, with an existential philosophy; they could not fit theology directly or indirectly into the structures of such a philosophy. Similarly, they had to become really serious and also burst into peals of laughter, just as they were enabled to become a little more human on that basis. They had no more use for irony. They no longer felt a need of, or a desire for, a state of suspension. Instead they were permitted to learn to walk. But for that they had to attend schools other than Kierkegaard's.

Thoughts on the 400th Anniversary of Calvin's Death

Whoever today commemorates the death of Calvin – he died in Geneva on 27 May 1564 – must make very sure that he has Calvin on his side in this matter and not against him. It was no coincidence that the place of his burial slipped into oblivion only a few years after his death. The monument to him and several other Calvinists of spiritual and secular standing of his time at Geneva was certainly not erected in his spirit. Calvin was no hero, and is not suited to hero-worship. Showing no trace of special consciousness of a prophetic mission, he desired to be merely the first servant of the Word of God for the Christian congregation at Geneva, as well as for others who came to him asking him to be that. He wanted, therefore, neither to be honoured nor applauded, nor even loved. Rather he wanted to be heard, simply as the witness to that to which he believed himself to be committed once it had won him for itself. Yes, there certainly were times when he insisted that he was right, times when he became passionate and even angry. Indeed, he was passionate and angry to the point of offensiveness; but never because it gave him pleasure. It was not for nothing that when he spoke of the order of the Christian's existence he placed almost all the emphasis on the teaching of the necessary mortification of the self in favour of God's self, God's will and pleasure. That is how he lived, a man who was ailing throughout his life and in his last years was very ill. That is how he died. And in this, as far as his person is concerned, he is to be respected.

Among the reformers Calvin is the leader of the second generation. This differentiates him from Luther and Zwingli. His spiritual home was the humanism of France, which had already come under the influence of German Protestantism. The world of his mature activity was on the one hand that of the Counter-Reformation, of which the most impressive high-points were in the first instance the founding and expansion of the Jesuit Order and in the second instance the deliberations and decisions of the Council of Trent, which went on for two decades. On the other hand, it was the onset of the modern age, manifested in the various philosophical, economic and political, but also aesthetic and religious, movements of the time. Calvin did his work within the framework of the encounter of these two mutually opposing but also deeply united elements of his age, and requires to be understood within them. He thought, acted and spoke for the renewal of the Church and its message on the basis of the Holy Scriptures; he thought, acted and spoke both for and against the self-affirming Christian Middle Age and Christian Antiquity, for and against just awakening modern man.

At the very beginning of his main literary work he wrote that the sum of all wisdom is the right knowledge of God and of man. The right knowledge of God is knowledge of him, not only as good and almighty, but as holy and also fatherly. The right knowledge of man is of man wholly dependent on God's free grace and revelation, of man who without God is lost in nothingness and really lives only in relation to God. Calvin's basic theme was, therefore, the history of God's covenant, the establishment of which is described in the Old Testament and the consummation of which is described in the New Testament, while it now moves towards its fulfilment; the covenant of God with men whom God has chosen, enlightened and sanctified through his Word in the power of the Holy Spirit. For them God's son became man, died, and rose again. God's community with them is the beginning and the aim of all his ways in creation and for creation. To exist in the obedience of faith under the law of his covenant of grace is the unending blessing and also the inviolable law and, therefore, the very meaning of their being. Their relationship to one another is constituted also by this law; their existence as the earth-bound people of God, serving his glory, moving on their pilgrimage toward the promised inheritance of eternal life.

This, very briefly, was the theology, the wisdom, that Calvin proclaimed. It is a wisdom which, as a first glance shows, was extremely practical and in its way extremely comforting, but above all it was extremely demanding. Calvin stood up for it in his century in his sermons, lectures and letters, qualifying here and defining there, and then drew it all together in the first, 1536, edition of his *Institutio Religionis Christianae* and then in the final 1559 edition.

The magnitude of his conception is reflected in the power, equally formative both psychologically and sociologically, which it has demonstrated in ever new guises, extending far beyond the few decades of his life, far beyond the small city of Geneva, far beyond Europe, and also far beyond the specifically ecclesiastical field. What today we call the 'Western' world, Western culture and civilization, would be unthinkable without it. You can, if you like, measure its magnitude also by the fact that, compared to its content, contours and dimensions, far too many later theological discussions, in the stricter sense of that word, right up to those of our own day, look like exchanges between pygmies, not to say fairy-tale dwarfs. What axiomatic certainty there is in the conception and execution of his task! What concentration on the one affirmation of the entire Holy Scripture, whichever way it is formulated! What a correlation of God and world, always daring but never divisive or confused; '*ubi cognoscitur Deus, etiam colitur humanitas*' ('where God is known, there humanity also comes into glory'), he once put it. What discipline of thought and language, restraining all arbitrarily roaming ideas! What direction of thought and instruction, always self-consistent and therefore reliable! What subjection to concrete service to which all thought and speech as such is directed! Something of the way of the divine-human event, documented in Holy Scripture, from which everything proceeds and towards which everything hastens, shines through in his work (which is so seldom the case in the works of man) and sustains it also in its human fragility and questionableness.

Calvin's authority was not the measure of all things for his more or less faithful successors, as Luther's became very early and still remains today for his successors. Everyone acquainted with Calvin's particular theological school soon discovers how seldom he is quoted in literature. Calvinistic orthodoxy (as well as the concept of 'Calvinism') was and is a contradiction in terms. You could, and can still today, only go to Calvin's school and learn from him. And because he wanted to direct his congregation, and with himself also his hearers and readers, to the school of the Holy Scriptures, the limits of his greatness and also the weaknesses of his strength had to and have to become visible and become serious problems in the instruction to be had from him.

However much he wanted to follow it, Calvin nevertheless violated the richness and depth of the prophets' and apostles' testimony. God's covenant of mercy with man could and should be, according to him, a covenant with a circle of certain people only, a covenant from the light and benefits of which he believed the vast majority to be excluded because of an inscrutable and unchangeable decision of God. Because of this, the distinction between the many who are evil and the few who are good and the purification of the congregation of all who only seemingly belong to it assumed an obviously improper predominance over the necessary distinction between good and evil. The notorious condemnation and execution of Michael Servetus and similar incidents come to mind here. Also the discipline of recruitment and of training of the true Christian was given an emphasis here the only effect of which could be unmistakably and undeniably to impose a certain atmosphere of gloom on the whole matter, against which all kinds of reactions became inevitable, both then and later. No one today should imagine that he would have been able to live in the Geneva ruled by Calvin with a good conscience, let alone with pleasure. It came to the point where he could not rid himself of a certain platonizing dualism in the categorization of the relationship between body and soul as well as of that between heaven and earth, things here and things beyond. It did not allow him to see and to bring into focus the totality of man's existence, his misery and also his redemption, a deficiency which necessarily brought a peculiarly life-denying coldness into his ethics and also, above all, into his hope for the future. He was undoubtedly stronger when he spoke about faith and obedience than about love and hope. Along this and other lines he was not only the child of his time, but also the prisoner of certain rigidities in his own basic ideas. From this vantage-point one understands the limits imposed on the truly deep and extensive influence of his life's work and not the least also on his ecclesiastical-ecumenical aspirations and strivings.

Yet, while seeing and admitting all this, it is impossible to shut one's eyes to the fact that, notwithstanding all the necessary criticisms and corrections, there is hardly a better teacher, apart from the biblical prophets and apostles, than he. Was it not he who once made the magnificent statement *'status mundi in laetitia Dei fundatus est'* ('the world's status rests in the joy of God')? And in another context: there is no element or particle of the world which in its affirmation of present misery is not 'oriented to the hope of its resurrection' (*'in spem resurrectionis intenta sit'*). Was it not he who unforgettably impressed on us the sovereignty of the gracious God over evil, and so also over the evil ones which we all are? Where, if not from him, can and must one learn that deadening law is the form and function of the life-giving Gospel, that God's demands are first and foremost his gift? By whom, if not by him, was the Christian congregation so energetically instructed that its existence is not an end in itself, that it should spread light and not gloom, that it should itself be light and as such serve God and do so in the obviously godless world? Calvin's conception as a whole is so thorough that it proves itself despite the less happy views in which he was not uncommonly involved. It is not worth while really to become a 'Calvinist', but it certainly is almost singularly worth while to become Calvin's free pupil. If today, after the experiences we have had of his life's work in its historical shape, and after a renewed return to the sources and origins to which he pointed so insistently, one can think and speak with him only by going beyond him in important areas, then one can fruitfully go *beyond* him only by thinking and speaking *with him* in the direction in which he pointed and do so looking back to the days of his work, his struggles and sufferings, in great reverence and genuine gratitude.

Karl Barth's Speech on the Occasion of his Eighteth Birthday Celebrations

Before we listen to the last strains of music this morning, may I say a word or two in reply? Several years ago I passed from the *ecclesia docens* to the *ecclesia audiens*, from the teaching to the listening Church. This morning I felt myself to be a member of the latter. And what have I had to listen to!

I approached this day with peculiarly ambiguous feelings, which overcame me again this morning as one after another of you came to the lectern to speak all those fine and beautiful words. I was torn between a sensation of great alarm and a great – yes, let me say so straight away – an even greater gratitude which has moved me during all these past weeks during which my name has appeared more and more frequently in mountains of newsprint and even on the bill-boards of this city. That is a terrifying thing, but it also inspires a deep gratitude. I do not want to cover up the fact that I was terrified then and that I have been terrified today, to this hour, terrified as a listener and terrified as the subject of so much that has been said. You see, what took place here today and in the papers during the past weeks ominously reminded, and still reminds me, of what Khrushchev – I almost said 'the blessed Khrushchev' – said of the era of his predecessor Stalin, that it had been an era of 'personality cult'. That is a dreadful thing, and it simply terrifies me that my name should continually have been appearing in the way it has been. Sometimes it has even appeared with odd epithets. I have seen it stated several times, for instance, that I have been and still am a great theologian. Elsewhere I have read even worse things from the pen of a friend of mine who is present here now, so I shall not mention his name. Fortunately he wrote what he did in a well hidden place, in the magazine of a Protestant congregation in the Near East which very few of you will ever get to see. With horror I read his statement that I was the greatest theologian of the century. That really terrified me, first of all because our century is not over yet, there are still thirty-four years to come. Who knows what little creature still wrapped in his diapers – or perhaps already wrapped in his theological diapers – will, when this century is looked back on, turn out to have been its greatest theologian, which I shall then turn out not to have been? What does the term 'greatest theologian' actually mean? When it finally becomes known who the greatest theologian of this century really was, perhaps it will turn out to be some little man or woman quietly engaged in Bible study somewhere on whom the light will shine. That is, if the ideas of 'greatness' and 'theologian' are compatible. In my last 'major' book, *Evangelical Theology: An Introduction*, I said explicitly that there may well be, let us say, great anatomists (such as our rector) or great musicians (such as Clara Haskil, especially when she plays Mozart's piano concertos), and so forth, but great theologians? That is a real contradiction in terms. As a theologian one can never be great, but at best one remains small in one's own way. Therefore this is not a good thing.

Then I read, and in our local church bulletin, that I am one of the Fathers of the Church. I thought with alarm of what Thomas Aquinas once said, that those who wore a halo in heaven fell into three categories, namely the holy martyrs, the holy virgins, and finally the holy teachers, who were none other than the Fathers of the Church. And now look at me. Do you detect anything about me remotely resembling a halo that I shall eventually win? I do not think so. From the very beginning of my theological work I have been very conscious of its relativity. For some strange reason, I have written evidence of this. As early as 1922,

SPEECH ON THE OCCASION OF HIS EIGHTIETH BIRTHDAY

when the star of the much heralded second edition of my *Epistle to the Romans* was just beginning to rise, I wrote an inscription on the fly-leaf of the author's copy. I have brought it with me today. I wrote it as if I were presenting a copy of the book to someone. But I presented it to myself, and what I wrote was 'From Karl Barth to his dear friend Karl Barth'. Then I added a few sentences I had just read in Luther. I propose to read them to you now, to explain what I had discovered then and what I now call my great alarm. The sentences from Luther were:

> If you think and are of the opinion that you really stand secure and you please yourself with your own books, your teaching and your writings, [if you think] that you have done very splendidly and have preached magnificently, and if it then pleases you to be praised before others, yes, if you perhaps want to be praised lest you mourn and give up, then, my friend, if you are man enough, put your hands to your ears, and if you do so rightly, you will find a lovely pair of big, long, rough donkey's ears. Do not spare the cost of decorating them with golden bells so that you can be heard wherever you go and the people can point to you and say: 'Behold, behold! There goes that splendid creature that writes such wonderful books and preaches such wonderful sermons.' Then you shall be blessed and doubly blessed in heaven, for the fire of hell is ready for the Devil and all his angels.

Thus wrote Luther. (For those of you who might like to refer to the text, it is in the Erlangen edition – at that time I did not possess a Weimar edition – Volume 63, and if I can still read it correctly, page 406.) That was the inscription I addressed to myself in 1922. And it has not changed in all these years and it has not changed today. Should this occasion today, and all these past weeks with the many beautiful things said about me, be a temptation to me, you may at least be aware that I am fighting a battle to resist it.

Excessive humility can, however, also be a form of arrogance. I had therefore better pass on to the next subject, my thanks. I have a very great deal to express my thanks for. First of all, I thank the organizers of this celebration, among whom my friend and colleague Max Geiger occupies a prominent place. He has spent a good part of his precious energy during the last quarter or nearly half year in preparation for today and all its details, especially last night's concert, which moved me very deeply.

I must thank everyone else too. I thank you for coming here – some of you from great distances – to say something kind to me. I have listened to all you have said, not only with trepidation, but also with real joy. I thank you too for the table of gifts laid out in various shapes. I shall look at them when I have returned home. I thank the musicians who have surrounded this day with so much beauty on the aesthetic side.

Then there is something very special calling for gratitude. It concerns one of the last speakers, my dear colleague Dr Koller, and not him only, but all the doctors who have cared for me at both the Bethesda and Bürger hospitals during the past two years during which I have been a pretty sick man. One of the doctors told me that in my present state, after that period of illness, I was not merely a success but indeed a triumph of modern medical science. Look at me and decide whether that is true. I feel, subjectively at any rate, that it is true. I cannot thank the doctors enough. But I do not have only them in mind, but also the orderlies, the deaconesses and the nurses at the Bethesda and the Bürger hospitals. They had great trouble with me, often very unpleasant trouble, but they cared for me faithfully day and night. I should not have been able to celebrate my eightieth birthday if all these doctors and their assistants had not done what they have done for me in the past two years.

Then, of course, I want to say thank you especially for the many honours which have been heaped on me today. Let me express my gratitude in the first place for the amazing honour I have received from Bonn, where I have been appointed to the position of an honorary senator. Mr Mayor of Bonn, you must first allow me to get used to that position. I have been wondering what the duties and privileges of such a senator may be – you will perhaps let me know – for the word 'senator' sounds very exalted, let alone 'honorary senator', which must be even more exalted.

Then I thank the Mayor of Basle for his vigorous speech here. I can assure both Mayors that I have got over certain disagreeable incidents that bothered me during my days in Bonn and Basle (in the latter particularly when I retired). As minister at Safenwil I grew a thick skin that came in handy in Germany, and later in Basle, so that not too many things 'got under my skin', and most just rolled off. So I bear no grudge against anyone, but recall with pleasure, with real pleasure, my days in Bonn, as well as those at Münster and Göttingen. But the days in Bonn were most interesting, because the waves were beginning to rise really high then, so that I felt quite well – in fact so well that it scared me a little – when I returned home to Basle, where the matters that engulfed me were more limited in scope than they had been in Bonn. But then I really had splendid times in Basle as a professor. So I thank the university, for which I did a few things. Twice I was nominated to become rector, but on both occasions I wriggled out. It was better for the university that I did so. Be that as it may, I thank you for everything given to me here. I should like to express thanks now for having been allowed to come to Basle. As it was, I was dismissed in Germany on a Saturday and on the following Monday the Basle Council offered me a professorship, so that I was out of work for that one Sunday only. I should like to underline the fact, and this will interest you all, that the two men who took the action which led to my call here were both declared atheists. It was the late *Regierungsrat* Hauser and the late *Ständerat* Thalmann who brought me here. *Dei providentia et hominis confusione Helvetia regitur* – that is how it was in those days.

There has been a great deal of talk today about my life-work and achievements. From my point of view, you know, the whole thing looks quite different from what you may suppose. I know myself better than you, or most of you, do. There are those depths, those relations and connections in my life which have not yet been mentioned: peculiar dispositions and aversions and the like. If my work for the Church, even for the world, has now been exalted, if all this recognition has been granted me all the way from the canton of Baselland to the Marxists of the German Democratic Republic, it is a great thing. But from my angle – I know my weaknesses. In a letter from my father, written when I was four (in 1890), I recently read the words: 'Karli again had to have the strap today.' I have had 'the strap' throughout my life, and perhaps more of it may still be in store for me, and that is what I really deserve more than all the fine things that have been said about me today. Let me again remind you of the donkey I referred to in connection with my *Epistle to the Romans*. A real donkey is mentioned in the Bible, or more specifically an ass. But let us call it a donkey. It was permitted to carry Jesus to Jerusalem. If I have done anything in this life of mine, I have done it as a relative of the donkey that went its way carrying an important burden. The disciples had said to its owner: 'The Lord has need of it.' And so it seems to have pleased God to have used me at this time, just as I was, in spite of all the things, the disagreeable things, that

SPEECH ON THE OCCASION OF HIS EIGHTIETH BIRTHDAY

quite rightly are and will be said about me. Thus I was used. I was on the spot – and while all these things were being said about me today I said to myself 'the battle was fought, the enemy struck, and there was I in the baggage-train'. That is how I happened to be present and that was my work. I just happened to be on the spot. A theology somewhat different from the current theology was apparently needed in our time, and I was permitted to be the donkey that carried this better theology for part of the way, or tried to carry it as best I could.

Let me conclude with two different quotations – the first in order once again to praise the medical people who have played such an important part in the last two years of my life. There is a passage in the Bible, though it is not in the actual Bible (may the representatives of the Catholic Church here forgive me), but in those books which, as Luther put it, are not to be put on a par with the Holy Scriptures, but are good and useful to read: the so-called Apocrypha. In Ecclesiasticus 38, there are several good passages; I shall not read the whole chapter, but merely the following: 'Honour a physician according to thy need of him with the honours due to him: for verily the Lord hath created him. For from the Most High cometh healing; and from the king he shall receive a gift. The skill of the physician shall lift up his head; and in the sight of great men he shall be admired.' Then it goes on: 'The Lord created medicines out of the earth; and a prudent man will have no disgust at them.' That is obviously a prophecy about the Basle pharmaceutical industry. I have been told that it substantially increased its dividends during my illness, for I had to make abundant use of its products. But listen to some more. It says of God that 'he gave men skill, that they might be glorified in his marvellous works. With them [the medicines] doth he heal a man, and taketh away his pain. With these will the apothecary make a confection.' And then 'there is a time when in their very

hands is the issue for good'. 'Let him not go from thee . .
for they also shall beseech the Lord.'

This is only a selection from that chapter. Read it
yourselves – Ecclesiasticus 38, dedicated to the faculty of
medicine by the faculty of theology.

I have overstepped the time-limit allotted for speeches;
I am well aware of that. Let me close with a verse of a
hymn, a verse of which I have always been especially fond.
I sang it with the students at Bonn when I had to take my
leave and again when I returned there in 1946. It is the
second verse from the famous hymn *Nun danket alle Gott*.
Let me say it now, not only for myself, but for you all.

> O may this bounteous God
> Through all our life be near us,
> With ever joyful hearts
> And blessed peace to cheer us;
> And keep us in his grace,
> And guide us when perplexed,
> And free us from all ills
> In this world and the next.

Letter to Eberhard Bethge

Dear Pastor Bethge,

It was very kind of you to send me the *opus grande* of your Bonhoeffer biography. After reading it with rapt attention from the first to the last page, I do not want to miss thanking you sincerely for this gift. It is a good, informative book. If I were asked whether one should buy it or not I would reply that one should indeed buy it. Several aspects of Bonhoeffer were new to me or have at least impressed themselves on me.

It was new to me that it was an early visit to Rome of all places that led Bonhoeffer to a living understanding of what the Church (and in the Church the institution of penance) might be, and that it was this which prompted him to leave the school of Seeberg, Harnack and Holl.

It was new to me above all else that Bonhoeffer was the first, yes indeed almost the only theologian who in the years after 1933 concentrated energetically on the question of the Jews and dealt with it equally energetically. For a long time now I have considered myself guilty of not having raised it with equal emphasis during the church struggle (for example in the two Barmen Declarations I composed in 1934). But then such a text would not have been acceptable either to the Reformed or the General Synod, given the spiritual predisposition of even the 'Confessing Christians' in 1934. But this does not excuse the fact that I (my interests lay elsewhere) did not offer at least formal resistance in this matter at that time. It was your book which made me aware that Bonhoeffer fought here right from the start. Then it was new to me that he considered going to India as seriously as you state. But why he wanted to do that is still not clear to me.

Also new to me was the idea that next to Bishop Bell I should have made and continued to make such an impression on him, until finally he thought it necessary to rebuke me with the concept of 'positivism of revelation', a concept still incomprehensible and unintelligible to me. So far I have always thought that I was no more than a 'pawn' and not at all a 'bishop' or even a 'rook' on his chessboard.

But more important than these or similar discoveries was the desire which I felt while reading your book to think over once again the unfinished road of your brother-in-law and friend in its entirety. I believe that one must distinguish between three lines, which for him were certainly inseparable but which in that inseparability are none the less not clearly drawn out for us (which is also true for your presentation and thus perhaps even for him too).

There is first of all what Herr Andreas Lindt calls Bonhoeffer's 'way from the Christian faith to political action' ('*Weg vom christlichen Glauben zum politischen Handeln*') in his recent essay in *Reformatio*. Exactly that, however, was also my concern after my farewell to theological liberalism. It took for me the form of 'religious socialism' in its specifically Swiss appearance.... When I began working on my *Epistle to the Romans* ... and after I went to Germany in 1921, this concern moved out of the centre somewhat. My German hearers and readers knew me better for the attempt of mine, which was more central to my thought, to give a new interpretation of the Reformation and to make it an actuality than for that other concern. Germany, burdened with the problem of her Lutheran tradition, was very much in need of a 'refresher course' in just the outlook which I presupposed without so many words and emphasized merely in passing, namely ethics, brotherliness (*Mitmenschlichkeit*), a servant Church, discipleship, Socialism, movements for peace – and throughout all these in politics. Obviously, Bonhoeffer sensed this void and the need to fill it with increasing urgency right from the start and gave expression to it on a very broad front. This overdue completion, for which he stood up so strongly, was and is (one hopes decisively) to a great extent the secret of the impression which he has justifiably made and is still making, especially since he became a martyr precisely for this cause.

Next to that the renewal of private and common worship which Bonhoeffer had in mind appears to be something different. I think I know what it is that he envisaged and I would draw it together in the concept of 'discipleship'. If this is in fact correct, I quite approve of the intention as such, although I must confess that your book does not make this completely clear to me. What he meant – was this the 'secret discipline' ('*Arkandisziplin*') of which he spoke at the end? – was obviously something different from the intentions of the Berneucheners and of Taizé. But what was it? As you know, his longing for India was highly perplexing to me. One would have to have been at Finkenwalde and involved like you in order to have a clear idea on this aspect. By the way, did Bonhoeffer arouse as much interest in this, did he have as many pupils or create such a precedent in this as he did in the matter just referred to?

Finally Bonhoeffer's views of the renewal of theology in both the narrower and wider senses of that term, the many-sided discussion of which was initiated and kept in high gear by his *Letters and Papers from Prison*, are something which is and remains a mystery to me even after having read your book. What is 'world come of age'? What does 'non-religious interpretation' mean? What am I to understand by the 'positivism of revelation' which he applied to me? I know everything, or certainly very much, of what the 'experts' including Heinrich Ott have made of these things. But thus far I do not know what Bonhoeffer *himself* meant and intended by all this and dare, therefore, to doubt gently that his real strength lay in theological systematics (I also have his *Ethics* in mind). Would he later not simply have dropped these *bons mots*? Was he really sure about what he meant when he composed them? But even if I am mistaken here, I still maintain that those letters from prison were only one, and indeed the last, of the stations of his life's way, which, right from the beginning, was a very lively spiritual venture. They certainly are not its goal. I would also maintain that he would have been capable of the most astounding evolutions in quite a different direction, and that one therefore does injustice to him – ranked all of a sudden in the same line as Tillich and Bultmann – to interpret him now on the basis of those passages (or to regard him as his own prophet in the light of them). It makes no difference whether this interpretation takes the form of an honestly bourgeois, new liberalism, whether it is made with Hanfried Müller as forerunner of the East German ideology, or with Regin Prenter as the new Lutheran Church father. It is unthinkable – and I put myself in his place now – what people would have done to me had I died a natural or violent death after the publication of the first or even the second *Epistle to the Romans* or after the appearance of my *Christliche Dogmatik im Entwurf* in 1927. What I would not have wanted to happen to me in such a case I would very much rather not have seen happening to Bonhoeffer.

Please, regard all these ruminations as a token of my thanks and of the attention with which I have read your book.

> With sincere greetings,
> Yours,
> Karl Barth.

Epilogue

The following address was given by the editor at the Memorial Service of the University of Toronto for Karl Barth in the chapel of Knox College on 19 December 1968.

A Thank-You to Karl Barth

We have gathered here this afternoon in this house of worship and of the study of the Word of God to pay our tribute to Karl Barth. Though the occasion for this service is his death, because it is he whom we commemorate, we should, indeed we can, set about it with gratitude and joy. For whoever commemorates this man must make sure to have him on his side. And to have Barth on your side means above all else to be joyful and glad – even on an occasion such as this.

If we wish to be faithful to this purpose, we shall not be able to make a 'graven image', even a verbal one, of him now. Any kind of monument to Barth would be contrary to his spirit. He was no hero, and is not suited to hero-worship. Two years ago, on his eightieth birthday, he chided the guests at the celebrations for having made the day into an occasion for something in the nature of a personality cult. He never showed any sense of possessing a special theological mission. He wanted to be no more than a servant of God's Word in the congregation. He wanted neither plaudits nor honours. He allowed us to love him as a man, but not as a theologian. As a theologian he wanted to be listened to, listened to as a witness to that which had won him over and to which he had committed himself. If some day somebody absolutely insists on donating a stained-glass window in his memory and wants to encircle his head with one of his famous sayings, let him choose his reply to a student at Richmond Theological Seminary in Virginia who asked him what the most momentous discovery of his long theological life had been: 'Jesus loves me, this I know, for the Bible tells me so.'

We shall have Barth against us if we speak of him as the greatest theologian of our century. That phrase really terrified him, he said in 1966, for in the first place there were still thirty-four years of the century to come. 'Who knows what little creature still wrapped in his diapers – or perhaps already wrapped in his theological diapers – will, when this century is looked back on, turn out to have been its greatest theologian?' he said. In his *Evangelical Theology: An Introduction* he calls the idea of 'greatness' incompatible with that of 'theologian'. As a theologian one could never be great, but at best one remained small in one's own way.

Therefore, my good friends, let us not, either today or tomorrow or at any other time, call him the greatest theologian of our age, or even a great theologian, for to do so would be contrary to his spirit. Nor let us call him the theologian most faithful to God's Word. That is not a judgment we are entitled to make, since, as Barth made plain to us, only God can make it.

But what shall we call him? We can, and therefore shall, call him the happiest theologian of our age. He was a joyful man, a man of humour. After all, he was a Basler, and Baslers, once you get to know them, really are as gay and as humorous as their carnival annually shows them to be. You can see Barth turning the laugh on himself when he says: 'The angels laugh at old Karl. They laugh at his trying to capture the truth about God in a book on dogmatics. They laugh, because volume follows volume, each thicker than the last, and as they laugh they say to

EPILOGUE

each other: "Look! There he goes with his barrow full of volumes on dogmatics." And they laugh at the men who write so much about Karl Barth instead of writing about what he is trying to write about.' Recently, in fact four days before his death, he told two friends that he had at last discovered the explanation of the size and number of his books. 'My doctors discovered that my colon was much too long', he said. 'Now at last I know why there is no end to my volumes on dogmatics.' This same humour, this same gift of God, which ranks just below the grace of God, was already evident in the younger, the 'dialectical', 'critical', 'diastatic' Barth. In 1922 he addressed to himself these words by Luther: 'If you think and are of the opinion that you really stand secure and you please yourself with your own books, your teaching and your writings, [if you think] that you have done very splendidly and have preached magnificently, and if it then pleases you to be praised before others . . . then, my friend, if you are man enough, put your hands to your ears, and if you do so rightly, you will find a lovely pair of big, long, rough donkey's ears. Do not spare the cost of decorating them with golden bells so that you can be heard wherever you go and the people can point to you and say: "Behold, behold! There goes that splendid creature that writes such wonderful books and preaches such wonderful sermons." Then you shall be blessed and doubly blessed in heaven, for the fire of hell is ready for the Devil and all his angels.'

Yes, Karl Barth was a joyful theologian, a happy theologian, a man who, because he was concerned with the Word of God (the *logos* of *theos*), could laugh. Theology, he said during his last term at Basle, was a happy, beautiful and liberating branch of knowledge: '*Theologie ist eine fröhliche Wissenschaft*', which I would translate as 'theology is a gay science'. The theologian who has no joy in his work is not a theologian, according to Barth. Morose faces, gloomy thoughts and boring ways of speaking are intolerable in this theology. (It should be pointed out that in German the term 'theologian' is extended to the priest, the bishop and the monk.)

Barth's humour is humour out of faith. A very appropriate academic and ecclesiastical honour to bestow on him would have been a doctorate *humoris causa*. His theology is marked by the syllable *eu* of the word *euangelion*. It is here, in the knowledge of faith in the power and finality of redemption, that man can laugh, laugh at himself, laugh in the happy expectation that the word of him who speaks the last word will most assuredly be a good word, a word infinitely better than all those muttered or spoken by man. Barth's humour is of the 'nevertheless' kind, like Mozart's music, in which the shadows of death and the dark hues of pain and suffering are not absent, but are nevertheless bathed in a radiance and harmony that sing praises to the goodness of God's creation.

'With Karl Barth's death an era has come to an end', some have said during recent days. I doubt very much whether that is true; Barth himself would be the first to take such people to task. My evidence again comes from his speech of thanks at his eightieth birthday celebrations. 'Let me again remind you of the donkey', he said when replying to the praises of his work. 'A real donkey is mentioned in the Bible, or more specifically an ass. But let us call it a donkey. It was permitted to carry Jesus to Jerusalem. If I have done anything in this life of mine, I have done it as a relative of the donkey that then went its way carrying an important burden. The disciples had said to its owner: "The Lord has need of it". And so it seems to have pleased God to have used me at this time, just as I was . . . I just happened to be on the spot. A theology somewhat different from the current theology was apparently needed in our time, and I was permitted to be the donkey that carried this better theology for part of the way, or tried to carry it as best I could.'

EPILOGUE

Barth's life has come to an end, yes, but has the carrying of a better theology therefore also come to an end? Has the time come to an end when it has to be said that, even though man may and indeed does let go of God, God does not let go of man? Did not Barth himself say that his *Church Dogmatics* was a tentative work, written only to be revised and refined by his students? The Karl Barth era will come to an end only when his students, and hopefully we are among them, give up going beyond him by continuing to think and speak with him in the direction in which he pointed. That era will come to an end when we refuse to be small donkeys that carry, or try as best as we can to carry, the testimony to God who, as the Bible tells us, loves us in Jesus Christ.

Permit me to conclude with a reference of a personal nature. I am the last Canadian who studied under Barth. After the end of his 'extra' term, the winter term of 1961-62, he visited America. On his return he again received his students in 'the upper room' at the Bruderholzhaus. I was to leave for home a week later, and felt sad at having to say what I thought was my final farewell. (Actually my wife and I met him again in 1964.) In any case, I managed to thank him for the immense enrichment, the encouragement and the joy, he had given me. He stood facing me in his black corduroy jacket, his glasses on the tip of his nose and his hair happily tousled. He put both hands on my shoulders, gave them a squeeze and said: 'Freely you have received, freely give.'

To us all, to the Church and to the world, Karl Barth gave his all freely. Therefore, thanks be to God for Karl Barth.

www.ingramcontent.com/pod-product-compliance
Lightning Source LLC
Chambersburg PA
CBHW050838160426
43192CB00011B/2067